Breaking the Code

Two teens reveal
the secrets to better
parent-child
communication

Breaking the Code

Lara Fox and
Hilary Frankel

 New American Library

New American Library
Published by New American Library, a division of
Penguin Group (USA) Inc., 375 Hudson Street, New York, New York 10014, USA
Penguin Group (Canada), 10 Alcorn Avenue, Toronto,
Ontario M4V 3B2, Canada (a division of Pearson Penguin Canada Inc.)
Penguin Books Ltd., 80 Strand, London WC2R 0RL, England
Penguin Ireland, 25 St. Stephen's Green, Dublin 2, Ireland (a division of Penguin Books Ltd.)
Penguin Group (Australia), 250 Camberwell Road, Camberwell, Victoria 3124,
Australia (a division of Pearson Australia Group Pty. Ltd.)
Penguin Books India Pvt. Ltd., 11 Community Centre, Panchsheel Park,
New Delhi - 110 017, India
Penguin Group (NZ), cnr Airborne and Rosedale Roads, Albany,
Auckland 1310, New Zealand (a division of Pearson New Zealand Ltd.)
Penguin Books (South Africa) (Pty.) Ltd., 24 Sturdee Avenue,
Rosebank, Johannesburg 2196, South Africa

Penguin Books Ltd., Registered Offices:
80 Strand, London WC2R 0RL, England

First published by New American Library,
a division of Penguin Group (USA) Inc.

First Printing, March 2005
10 9 8 7 6 5 4 3 2 1

NEW AMERICAN LIBRARY and logo are trademarks of Penguin Group (USA) Inc.

LIBRARY OF CONGRESS CATALOGING-IN-PUBLICATION DATA
Fox, Lara.
Breaking the code : two teens reveal the secrets of better parent-child communication /
Lara Fox and Hilary Frankel.
p. cm.
ISBN 0-451-21418-8 (trade pbk.)
1. Parent and teenager. 2. Communication in the family. 3. Interpersonal
communication in adolescence. I. Frankel, Hilary. II. Title.
HQ799.15.F69 2005
306.874—dc22   2004021867

Set in Plantin
Designed by Patrice Sheridan

Printed in the United States of America

Dedicated to our biggest fans, our parents.

Names have been changed to protect the innocent.

Acknowledgments

Alice Martell, thank you for giving us the confidence and motivation to keep pushing. Without your incredible dedication and encouragement, we would have given up a long time ago. Whenever we doubted ourselves, you were always there to reassure us that the teenage point of view needed to be heard. Thank you for taking a risk on two inexperienced teenagers and treating us like adults.

To Howard Mittelmark: We've resisted for a year now, but we can't any longer. . . . Howie, thanks for being a total cheeseball and making sure that we stayed honest and true to the teenage voice. More important, thanks for making sure we got that monkey in the book. We really loved working with you, and we are sure that you loved talking to us late on Saturday nights—even if you won't admit it. Thank you for always keeping us in check.

To Stacey and Deborah, thanks for breaking the parents in for us. Your past experiences as teenagers have helped us to see parent-teen relationships from an outside perspective. Thanks for taking the time out of your busy college-student lives to give us a call and ask how it's going. Your support as sisters has really helped us to survive the teenage years.

To the rest of our families, thanks for always showing interest in this project, which has been such a big part of our lives. Every bit of encouragement has helped.

Oh, Nancy (Ms. Fried), if not for your nosiness, this book would not be more than an idea. Thank you for your constant support, weekly pep talks/checkups, and extreme leniency.

To all our friends, thank you for being our best distraction and support system. Without you guys we wouldn't have had such a tremendous amount of material to work with.

To Tracy Bernstein, thank you for your patience and your confidence in two clueless teenagers. You've really made this process a positive one for us.

Finally, to the leading characters in this book: (Mom and Dad)^2, Lynn & David, Jan & Steven, we know that we have been quite a handful this past year and a half, but we really appreciate your constant love and enthusiasm for this project and for us. This project wouldn't have been possible without such positive and strong relationships with you guys. Thanks for being our biggest cheerleaders and teaching us to channel our frustration into something more constructive. You've made this experience special every step of the way.

Contents

Introduction   1

1.   "No Trespassing!":
Respecting Personal Privacy   5

2.   "Just Accept it—I'm *Not* Going to Harvard!":
Surviving High School with Your Teen   43

3.   "But Everyone Else Is Going!":
Curfew and Other Issues That Go
Bump in the Night   93

4.   "I Wish I Were an Only Child!":
Brothers, Sisters & Friends   139

5.   "I Want You to Express Yourself,
but Take That Shirt Off!":
Clothing, Tattoos and Piercing   179

6.   "Money *Doesn't* Grow on Trees?":
Teen Finance   211

Afterword   241

Introduction

This probably isn't the first parenting book you've ever bought. If you've made it to the teenage years, you've probably been through a few. Maybe you even bought baby books when you first became a parent. Those books were a real help because babies can't talk, so you didn't know what they were thinking, and you needed the experts to tell you what was going on in their soft little heads. Then your kids grew up and started talking and everything got easier. They could tell you where it hurt, and why they were sad, and what would make them happy. Now you realize that was just a phase.

You knew there was something familiar about having a teenager, didn't you? Our heads are harder, but once again, you don't know what's going on in them. And once again, you need expert help. That's where we come in.

We're here to tell you how teenagers think and how they interpret the things you say. This book will guide you through your teenager's thought process and teach you how to improve the interactions you have with your teenager so both of you can communicate more effectively.

Maybe you thought you were making great progress in communication, and it turned out your teenager was plotting how to avoid seeing you all weekend. Maybe you find yourself tiptoeing around your teenager, out of fear that anything you say will piss her off and she won't talk to you for a week.

Just remember, sometimes there's no rhyme or reason, no method to our teenage madness. We just react, and unfortunately, there's nothing you can do to help. We know that this is a really hard concept for you as parents to accept because you remember when things were so much easier. But things have changed. Your teenager is pushing you away more and more and you're dying to know why. This book does not encourage you to look through your teen's backpack in order to find out why; it does, however, show you how to talk to your teen so she will feel more comfortable talking to you about what's going on in her life.

Teenagers constantly misinterpret what their parents say, and that's one of the reasons they keep so much to themselves; they think their parents have ulterior motives. We'll show you what your teen will be receptive to and what will just make him even more distant.

Each chapter of this book deals with an area where things can go really wrong when you talk to your teen, like personal privacy, or school, or money. We show you scenes (from our own lives, and our friends' lives) that demonstrate common ways things do go wrong, and then we follow up with scenes showing your best approach for fixing them (or avoiding the mess in the first place).

This book will not provide a script that you can recite when you are talking to your teen; it's a guide to what teens *really* hear when you speak, and how you can make them hear what you are actually trying to say. You'll quickly see how teenagers dissect and add meaning to even the most innocent thing you say. Hopefully, this will help eliminate the petty fights that are based on miscommunication. This doesn't mean you won't fight with your teen. Fights *will* happen—in fact, sometimes you want them to happen, because that's often how you finally find out what's really going on. It's healthy. The goal is to keep the bloodshed to a minimum.

Chapter 1

"No Trespassing!":

Respecting Personal Privacy

"Get out!"

Sound familiar? Well, don't take it personally. For a teen, making parents "get out" is part of growing up. As you've probably figured out by now, we teenagers are moody and demanding, but when we start demanding our privacy, it's not just because of our moods.

We made the first chapter of our book about privacy for a reason. Nothing is more important to a teenager than starting to get the respect we think we deserve. We're not kids anymore, even though you think we still act like kids sometimes. We know we're not adults either, even though we say you should treat us like adults. What are we? We are people who are *learning how* to be adults, and one of the ways we do this, a really important way, is by becoming more private. The first place we do this is at home, and the biggest part of it, we're sorry to have to be the ones to tell you, is going to be shutting you out.

This is probably upsetting to you right now. Being the parent of a teenager can be an upsetting thing, because everything is changing. You can remember the days when you were the whole world to your kids. Their lives revolved around you, and you were part of all their important decisions, and at the end of the school day they would come home and tell you everything that happened. It was like you had a backstage pass to your children's lives.

Now the best you can hope for is a seat out in the audience, and it probably won't even be a very good seat. From there, it can be hard to figure out what's going on with your kids, and it's hard to tell when teenagers want and need you to get involved in their world.

That's where we come in: we live in their world, and we can give you an inside look; we know what teenagers want and when they want it, and we can also tell you when it isn't the best thing for them to get what they want.

Before we even start that, though, here is the first thing you should keep in mind before entering the teenage world: Remember that annoying friend from back in high school? You know, the one that constantly wanted to spend time with you and always called to see what you were doing? The one that tried to go wherever you were going, and join your new crowd, even though it was obvious they didn't belong? That is how your teen sees you now. You aren't the cool, hip friend. You aren't the smart or trustworthy friend. You're the annoying friend.

The thing is, teenagers don't need or want another hip friend. We need someone who cares about us, someone who wants to know where we are because they're concerned about our safety, not because they want to come hang out with us.

Your teens still want to be invited out with you because it reminds them that they always have a place with you, even though they'll rarely accept the invitation. And there's the thing that can get confusing. Teenagers want to be treated like adults, and they'll snap at you if they detect you treating them like children. But at the same time, they need to know that you're still there, looking out for them; that you're still the parent.

Basically, you can't win. Let's all admit that right now. No matter what you do, your teenager is going to have a problem with it. But with our help, you can understand your teenager better, and make things less painful than you could on your own.

His Room Is His Castle

One of the first things you can do to make things easier for everyone is respect your teen's personal privacy. You'll "get away with" a lot more of the things that bug us if we know that you respect us, and that's probably the best way to do it. If you respect our privacy just like you would an adult's, it tells us that you know we're not just kids anymore—and what you think of us really matters, even if we don't show it all the time. Or ever.

"UNLOCK THIS DOOR!"

It's seven o'clock and Amy, Sasha's mother, wants to know whether Sasha and her friend Colin are staying in for the evening. Amy attempts to open Sasha's door and finds that it's locked. Amy immediately becomes suspicious of her daughter's relationship with Colin. She begins to knock violently on her daughter's bedroom door. There is no response; instead she hears the slow turn of the lock. It's obvious that Sasha was trying to hide that the door was locked to begin with. The music had been so loud that she didn't hear Amy's first attempt to enter the room.

"Why is the door locked?"

"It wasn't. Why does it matter, anyway? We're just listening to music. What do you want?"

"I know the door was locked. I tried to open it!" screams Amy.

"Haven't you ever heard of knocking?" Sasha mumbles under her breath.

"I have had enough of your attitude! When you live under my roof, you abide by my rules. You can't go out tonight."

"What? That's outrageous! Who do you think you are?"

"I am your mother and your friend needs to go home. Don't even think about blaming me for this one; you ruined your own night." Sasha rolls her eyes and slams the door in Amy's face while asking Colin to turn the music up.

Sasha was obviously out of line, but the door probably wouldn't have been locked if she understood why her mother felt so strongly about the no-locked-doors rule. Your teen is going to resist the rules you make and try to argue about them. Your only chance of etching this type of rule into your teens' heads and making it stick is if they understand your reasoning. Maybe they won't agree with you, but they still need to understand.

In the case of a locked door, the best reasoning you can give for the rule is "if you have nothing to hide, then there's no reason to lock the door. We're more than willing to give you your personal space, we just feel more comfortable with the door open." Although they may not admit it, teens know that this is extremely reasonable and fair.

But there's more going on in this situation than just the locked door. The first thing that went wrong was when Amy started screaming and losing control at the door. Hey, we know we can drive you crazy, but the fact is if you freak out there isn't much chance that a teen's reaction will be positive, especially with a friend (and *especially* with a *boy* friend) witnessing everything. After the door was finally opened, Amy should have postponed the discussion about the door being locked. If she was worried that Sasha might do it again, she could have asked to speak with Sasha in private to avoid embarrassing her even more.

Part of parenting is anticipating a teenager's reaction. Maybe if Colin weren't there for the conversation, Sasha wouldn't have been so disrespectful. As Amy was speaking to Sasha, Sasha wasn't hearing a word her mother was saying; it was going in one ear and out the other. Instead, Sasha was focused on the impression it was leaving on Colin.

The mistake on Sasha's part was when she chose to lie about the door being locked. This lie probably sprouted from being embarrassed that her parents wouldn't permit her door to be locked in the first place. Colin was there, listening to every word, so Sasha wanted to avoid an argument, and she wanted to avoid looking childish in front of Colin. No teen wants to explain the "strange" rules in her house, and although Colin probably has a few at his house, Sasha wasn't thinking about that. She was just in a rush to get her mother out of her room without being humiliated.

Sasha interpreted each of her mother's actions as another attempt to embarrass her; Sasha doesn't see it for what it was, a conversation about the rules. When Amy said, "Why is the door locked?" Sasha *heard*, "I don't trust you" or "You're not mature enough to have the door locked."

What would help a lot is if Amy did something to show that she did respect Sasha's privacy, even if she doesn't let her lock the door. Like most teens, Sasha would appreciate it if her parents knocked before entering her room. Teens are so adamant about this because they feel it sets up a system of privacy. Although a knock may seem insignificant and unimportant, it not only makes us feel respected, it makes us feel like *our* room is really ours. Your teen would be more willing to follow the no-locked-doors rule if she knew a knock would replace the lock.

"GO TO YOUR ROOM."

Colin has just arrived home from Sasha's. Unfortunately, he forgot to call and tell his parents he wouldn't be home for dinner. Not realizing the trouble he's in, Colin skips the hellos and goes straight to the den to watch the end of a baseball game.

Having heard the front door slam a few minutes before, Colin's mother, Deborah, comes into the den and asks sharply, "Why didn't you call?"

Not understanding the seriousness of the matter at first, Colin ignores his mother and continues watching the intense replay of the latest run scored. Already disappointed, his mother shuts off the television and says, "Colin, go to your room."

Colin knows he was wrong not to call, but naturally he is frustrated that he is going to miss the last few minutes of the game. So he throws down the remote control and walks off to his bedroom, muttering under his breath, "Bitch." Colin slams the door behind him and flops down on his bed.

Insulted and angry, Deborah bursts into Colin's room, ready to reprimand him.

"Get out! This is *my* room! You sent me here, remember?"

"Don't ever call me a bitch again. Show some respect. I'm your mother."

"Sorry," grumbles Colin. "Can you leave now?"

"No, I'm not finished yet."

"You sent me to my room and I listened. Now would you please remove yourself from *my* room?"

"Every room is my room, Colin. This is my house. I bought it. So as long as you're under my roof, you will listen to what I have to say." Satisfied with her response, Deborah leaves the room.

The problem with a scene like this is that it makes teens feel like they have their own space and privacy one minute and it's being snatched away from them the next. A consistent sense of personal space and privacy, with a distinct set of guidelines and regulations, is essential for teenagers to develop their independence. When parents start to change the understanding of terms like "your room," teens become confused about what is and is not theirs, and they lose the structure they need.

It's true that Colin shouldn't have come home late without calling, ignored his mother, or showed disrespect by calling her a bitch, but in his mind these actions are insignificant in comparison to his mother's. Colin interprets the situation like this: his mother contradicted herself by barging in when it's supposed to be *his* room, invading his space just to get the

---

TIP

Teens need to have the last word. When Colin said "bitch" under his breath, it was his way of ending the conversation in his favor. For teens, having the last word is a way of saving face. Unfortunately, it's up to parents to bite their tongues and walk away *for the moment*, because it's guaranteed that their teens will not, and one of you needs to be the grown-up.

We're not asking you to brush off the comment—teens need to know that calling their mother a bitch is inappropriate and will not be tolerated under any circumstance. But it would be in your best interest to walk away and give your teen the last word. Wait until you've both cooled off, and then you can approach the issue calmly and be more effective.

---

upper hand and get in the last word. Colin thinks that if his mother is willing to invade his space this time, then she won't hesitate to take away all his personal privacy. Therefore, there's no reason for him to do what she tells him the next time.

"CLEAN YOUR ROOM RIGHT NOW!"

Claire is sitting at her desk on a Wednesday evening typing to a bunch of friends online. Her mother, Lucy, comes into the room without knocking. She takes one look and sees dirty clothes piled up all over the floor, stray papers and crumpled tissues lying around, empty soda cans that have missed the garbage, and an unmade bed . . . among other things.

"Claire, get off that computer right now and clean this room up. It's absolutely disgusting."

"Don't you knock?" Claire grumbles.

"Your room is a pigsty!"

"I'll clean it later." Claire continues to type without even looking away from the computer screen.

"No, you'll do it *now*."

"Chill out, Mom."

"I am chilled out, Claire, but this is just ridiculous. I try not to get involved in your business, but this has gone too far. You have no respect for things I buy you. You just leave them on the floor and don't even attempt to keep this room the least bit clean. I've had enough."

"This is *my* room and it's really none of your business how I keep it, so just let me handle it myself for once. Now would you please get out?"

"This might be your room, but this is my house. I work long days so you can enjoy a nice house and have your own room. Now I think it's your turn to show some respect and keep it clean, like a civilized human being. Besides, why would you want to live in a filthy room?"

"Mom! Please! You are *so* frustrating. I can't deal with this right now. I'll clean it later, just please get out, you're really starting to bug me."

A quick note before getting to the main subject: even though Claire doesn't make a big deal out of it, Lucy really needs to learn how to knock. It might seem like an insignificant gesture, because your teen almost always says you can come in, but it shows respect for your teen and her privacy, and if you want respect when you ask her to clean her room then you need to show her respect in return. If you haven't knocked, and then you say, "Clean your room," you're asking for your teen to ignore you. Teens want to be treated like adults; we no longer keep the door open all the time, like we did when we were little, and there's a reason: we want privacy and we want you to respect it, just like you would respect any other person's privacy.

Now, the main issue. Who decides the way a teenager's room is kept? The bedroom is the most personal place a teenager has because it is the only space that is truly her own, even if she shares it with a sibling. The teenager sees it as her choice when and when not to clean her room, how to clean it, and all the other decisions relating to the bedroom. That's where the dilemma comes in. Mom thinks that Mom has control and Claire thinks that Claire has control.

In this situation, the problem is that Lucy was pushed over the edge. She has probably been wanting to say something to Claire about the condition of her room for days, so now she is letting all her frustration out at once, in an irrational manner. By bursting into the room and ordering her daughter to clean up, Lucy is making the situation more difficult for herself. She is guaranteeing right off the bat that her daughter won't want to listen to her or do anything she is told to do. Claire is probably thinking, "Screw you. I'm in the middle of something that's important to me, and cleaning my room can wait. I said I'll do it, so just go away."

To actually get your teen to clean her room, you have to find a different approach. For example, instead of making demands, you could make it a suggestion, or make a joke out of it. Ordering teens to clean their rooms, or threatening them (e.g., saying they can't go out until their room is clean), makes teens absolutely *not* want to clean. If they don't respond to your more reasonable requests, *then* you can come in and make threats.

A threat like "You can't go out tonight until your room is clean" will probably work, but it's unfair if you haven't given your teen a warning a day or two before. Chances are Claire will be thinking, "What a jerk. She thinks she can threaten me now, but she won't have that control over me forever. I'll just shove the clothes under the bed, and that old hag will never figure it out. She thinks I'm stupid, but *she's* really the stupid one." Keep in mind that she'll be angry if you threaten her in any way or at any time, no matter how much you've warned her, but the room *will* get cleaned.

Also, by the way, your teen knows when her room is messy—she isn't oblivious. It's just that if it doesn't bother her to live in a disorganized room, then she'll see no point in spending the time and energy cleaning up. That's why no matter what you say, it probably won't happen until she becomes fed up and can't live in the mess any longer.

The things you say really won't get the job done; at most it will probably just start to bug her, especially if you make a comment every time you come in her room. Really, you shouldn't make a big deal out of this issue. It's not going to hurt anyone if your teen lives in a messy room. Also, it doesn't help you to make it a bigger issue than it is. Teens will take you less seriously the more fights you pick with them. You never want your teen to be thinking, "Oh, here she goes again"; you want your teen to take you seriously.

Another reason your teen won't respond to demands like Lucy's is because she sees the room as *hers*. A teen's room is an intensely private place and she doesn't think you have any right to tell her when she should clean up, or how she should be behaving in her room in general. When you barge in and demand these things, your teen feels like her privacy has been invaded.

Here's another approach, which could lead to less grief.

> "Claire, I know you are busy right now, but do you think you could clean your room? We are having company over tomorrow."
>
> "Why does it matter? The Kutnicks know what a teenager does. What's the point in pretending I'm a neat person?"
>
> "Okay, fine. Don't do it for them—do it for me."
>
> "I don't want to."
>
> "Well, that's not really an option. I'm not saying you need to do it right now, but it needs to be cleaned up by tomorrow."

Yes, teens are snotty. Lucy approached it perfectly and Claire still found some way to insult her and make her feel bad. Either way, Claire gets the clear message that she needs to clean her room. In this scenario, Lucy has found an effective approach—she doesn't say Claire has to do it right now; she acknowledges that this isn't Claire's priority, and that it's okay to do it on her own schedule as long as it's done by tomorrow.

Your teen understands why you want her to clean, even if she gives you a hard time. If it turns out that Claire hasn't cleaned her room by the morning, then Lucy must step in and gently remind her. Your teen may have genuinely forgotten—we know we have, because it isn't at the top of *our* list—so keep that in mind before you get worked up about it.

It's My Body, But You'll Pry If You Want to

As teens grow up, it's not just our rooms that we feel are our private business. Once upon a time, we came running to you whenever we got a scrape or a bump, but as teenagers we feel more private about our bodies, too, and we need you to respect that.

It's Private. Period.

THIS COULD HAVE GONE BETTER

Lindsay is twelve years old and in seventh grade. It is a Wednesday morning. Her mother, Loraine, has just woken her up for school and led her groggily into the bathroom. As Loraine is leaving the bathroom, she hears Lindsay call out for her in a panicked voice. Loraine comes back into the bathroom.

"Lindsay? What is it?"

"Oh my God. Mom, I think I got my period. . . ." Lindsay has a mixture of horror and excitement on her face, but she is mostly just surprised.

"Oh, Lindsay! Congratulations! That's so exciting, honey. Right?"

"I guess. . . ." Lindsay begins to cry.

"What's wrong?"

"I don't know. . . . What am I supposed to do? I don't want to go to school. I'm not going to school."

"Don't be silly, Lindsay. I have to get to work. Let me show you what to do, and then you better get in the shower because we're going to be late." Loraine takes out the supplies she bought for Lindsay a couple of months before and quickly explains things.

"Mom?"

"Yes, Lindsay?"

"Don't tell Dad."

"All right, Lindsay, whatever. You have got to get moving. I have an early meeting."

"I'm going, I'm going. Wait—Mom?"

"Yeah?"

"What am I supposed to tell my friends?"

"I don't know. Don't tell them anything. What's the big deal? Come on, we can talk more later. I have to finish getting ready."

The problem here is that Loraine is completely insensitive to everything that Lindsay is going through. It is obviously understandable if Loraine can't be late, but she could slow down for a minute and help Lindsay get through this. When Lindsay says not to tell her father, Loraine brushes the comment aside. When Loraine says, "All right, whatever," she may mean "Okay, I promise," but Lindsay hears, "I don't care whether or not you want Dad to know. I don't care about your feelings." Because she doesn't understand that it's something really important and private to Lindsay, there is much more of a chance she'll let it slip to her husband.

Lindsay is distressed by the whole situation and Loraine isn't helping; in fact, she might be hurting Lindsay by her lack of concern. To Lindsay this is a *big* deal. When Lindsay asks what to tell her friends, Loraine doesn't give her the time of day; she doesn't even seem to notice that it is something her daughter is worried about.

For a teenage girl, whether it is something she has wanted or not, getting her period is a monumental event. When her parents brush it aside and don't really take the time to help her through it, it makes her feel like her parents don't care about how she is feeling.

A LITTLE UNDERSTANDING
GOES A LONG WAY

Loraine comes back into the bathroom when she hears Lindsay.

"Lindsay? What is it?"

"Oh my God. Mom, I think I got my period. . . ." Lindsay has a mixture of horror and excitement on her face, but mostly she is just surprised.

"Oh, Lindsay! Congratulations! That's so exciting, honey. Right?"

"I guess. . . ." Lindsay begins to cry.

"What's wrong?"

"I don't know. . . . What am I supposed to do? I don't want to go to school. I'm not going to school."

"All right, it's okay. You can be late if you want. Let me explain this. . . ." Loraine takes out the supplies she bought for Lindsay a couple of months before, and together they go over things.

"Mom?"

"Yes, Lindsay?"

"Don't tell Dad."

"Why not?"

"Because!"

"Okay, I won't."

"And, Mom, what am I supposed to tell my friends?"

"You don't have to tell them anything at all. Nobody will know—it's completely private. It's up to you if you want to tell them."

"So nobody can tell?"

"Nope, not at all. They'll only know if you tell them. Right now it might be something you feel embarrassed to talk about with your friends, but soon enough all you girls are going to be in the same boat, making jokes and complaining about it together. It's something we all go through. I know it might seem unlikely now, but it becomes much easier to talk about after a while."

"Maybe . . ."

"I promise, Lindsay."

This was obviously a very mixed experience for Lindsay. She was shocked because it came unexpectedly, excited because it's something all women go through, and nervous because it's something new and she couldn't understand what it would really be like, no matter what she's heard.

For some girls it will be much less upsetting; they might be totally prepared for it and thrilled when it happens. Because it can be a very confusing event, it's extremely important that Loraine is as sensitive as possible to Lindsay. When Lindsay asks if she can stay home from school, Loraine doesn't just dismiss it, she takes the time to reassure her that it's something personal and private and nobody's business but hers, and that her day at school won't be any different than usual. In this case, Loraine was even sensitive to Lindsay needing more time than usual to get ready and reassured her that it was okay to be late.

If your daughter is excited, get excited with her. If she's upset, it doesn't help to be upset with her, but you can try and make a joke out of it. Tell her you know what a pain it is to try to cheer her up.

One thing you don't want to do is make her feel like she's overreacting. This is probably one of the most bizarre things she is going to go through as a teenager, and any response she has is valid.

If you say something like "Oh, come on. It's not the end of the world. We all have to go through it," she hears, "Stop being a baby." It can come off as condescending, and your daughter may feel like you think she is immature or that you just don't understand her feelings. It's much better to joke around, saying "I know we all have to go through it and it sucks, but hey, at least it's only once a month!"

If she really doesn't seem to want to talk about it, you don't need to dwell on it. If your daughter just wants to forget it, then talk about something else. Take her out to dinner later, rent a movie, have fun. If your daughter doesn't want to make it a big deal, then you shouldn't either. If she does, you've got to be right there with her.

Things can be even more sensitive if your daughter gets her period much earlier than all her friends, or if she is on the other extreme and gets it *after* all her friends. If she is early, then she might be more embarrassed to tell you or her friends because she has nobody else her age to relate to and it separates her from all her friends. If she gets it late she can feel like she hasn't matured yet and will really want to get her period so she can fit in. A major part of what determines how your daughter feels about getting her period is where she is in relation to her friends and the other girls at school. Like so many things in middle and high school, it's about fitting in. Nobody ever wants to be on the outside, and getting your period at a particular time can make you feel like that.

Anything that happens to someone's body is their own business, and they get to say how private they want to be about it. For teenage girls, getting your period is a particularly touchy and personal issue. This was evident with Lindsay;

she was worried other kids would know and she didn't want Loraine to tell her father. Many girls will tell only their mothers and their best friends, or maybe another friend who has already gotten her period.

Every girl feels slightly different about menstruation and cares about different aspects. It's important to listen carefully to what your daughter says, because that's the only way you'll know what *her* response is. For example, if she says, "Don't tell Dad," that doesn't just mean she doesn't want her father to know, it's a sign that she doesn't want you to announce it to the world in general. She probably wants you to treat the whole thing in a fairly low-key manner, in which case you have to respect that.

One thing Lindsay's mother said that's really important, especially for girls who aren't excited to get their period, is, "I know it might seem unlikely now, but it becomes much easier to talk about after a while." For those of us who, for whatever reason, aren't happy about it, or don't even want it to happen, it is nice to be assured by someone who went through it that it becomes much easier with time.

You might even want to acknowledge that you went through it quite a while back. If you do, remind your daughter that all women in every time have gone through it and it's something we can *all* understand. This will help her realize that your advice isn't completely dated and she can trust you about such important issues.

YOU WANT FRIES WITH THAT FOOT, DAD?

Lindsay is in her room doing her math homework.
Her father has just returned home from work and comes into her room.

"Congratulations, Lindsay."

"What?"

"You know, congratulations, on . . . that," he says again, somewhat uncomfortably.

"Thanks." Lindsay turns away, fighting back tears. After her father leaves, she yells for her mother. Loraine comes to Lindsay's room.

"What's up?"

Lindsay is crying. "I can't believe you! You told Dad and I told you *not* to do that. What the hell? Are you crazy? Jeez!"

"I'm sorry. He asked why you were going to school late and it just came out. I shouldn't have—"

"No, you shouldn't have. I can't believe you. Now how am I supposed to trust you if I know you're going to turn around and tell Dad? You probably tell the whole world everything I tell you."

"I'm sorry, Lindsay. I messed up."

"Get out. I can't talk to you now."

"I know you don't want to hear me explain myself, honey, but he is really excited for you and I'm sorry I broke my promise. I've never repeated anything you've told me privately and I will never do that again."

"Whatever, Mom."

So, your cover is blown. Parents tell each other *everything*. It doesn't matter whether or not your teen asks you not to tell, you work as a unit. But your spouse slips up once and your covert operation is over. She now knows you guys can't keep a secret.

It's pretty devastating the first time we realize that you're telling each other just about everything we tell you. Even if you *haven't* told your husband or wife some of the little things, it doesn't matter; you broke your teen's trust once and now she thinks you have never kept it.

This is an issue of personal privacy. When teens tell you something in confidence, they expect you to keep it a secret. When you don't, your child feels completely violated. The first time is the worst, and then they eventually realize that it makes sense that you are working together and sharing information with each other.

After your teen finds out, it's important to talk to them about it. In the future, there may be things that they want to tell you, but they won't if they feel they can't really completely trust you. If and when your teen becomes sexually active, she'll need to be able to trust you one hundred percent if she's going to talk to you about it. That's not going to happen if you have a trust issue looming from the time you told your spouse who your daughter's fifth-grade boyfriend was.

This means you have to go back to your teen after she has cooled down a little and explain to her why you told your spouse. Saying something like "It just slipped out" isn't going to help, even if it's the truth. To you it may mean "It was a complete accident. I didn't set out to hurt you," but what your teen will hear is "Your secret wasn't important enough to me to really pay any attention to your wishes, and obviously I don't respect your privacy, but get over it because I don't think it's a big deal."

When a teen tells you to keep something a secret, assume that it must be a big deal in her eyes, or else she wouldn't tell you to keep it quiet. Letting it "slip out" is discrediting the importance of her feelings.

You need to admit you made a mistake and apologize for that, but *also* explain that you *do* understand the importance of her feelings. You should do whatever is necessary to make sure she understands that in the future you won't betray her trust, assuming her safety isn't at risk. This might also be a good time to explain that there are certain things you *can't* keep a secret from her other parent. This way, she understands what you will and won't repeat so she can make the decision if she wants to tell you something.

In this particular situation, it might be a good idea for Loraine to tell Lindsay that although she was wrong in telling her husband, Lindsay should know that her father wants to know what's going on in her life, and he was just excited for her. Lindsay should know that it's understandable to feel embarrassed, but she doesn't need to, and doesn't need to keep it a secret, either, because it's something her dad wants to celebrate with her. This will help her see that her father is also interested in her maturation, that he's excited for her and wants to be involved in her life. This can only make her feel good; it can never hurt to be reminded that her father loves her.

One last word of advice. It was a *really* bad move for Lindsay's father to say something if he knew he wasn't supposed to know. Although in the end it's good for your teen to know the truth about parent-to-parent communications, it would have been much better if he had waited until Loraine had told her daughter, "There are some things I *have* to tell Dad," or asked her, "Are you sure I can't tell your dad? I think he would be really interested and excited." The more you actually discuss things in situations like this, the less sneaking around there will have to be, and the fewer explosive arguments leading to somebody losing somebody else's trust.

Your Teen Is Not Invisible

We know we don't have the right to hear or know about everything that goes on in your life, but you can't expect us not to ask. So, if you are going to talk about personal things in front of us, make sure that you are willing to dish out the details; at the least, expect that an interrogation will follow. This means you can't start up a conversation with your spouse or the person sitting next to you if you aren't willing to share the story with all the kids who are present at the table. It's pretty simple. If you don't want us to know, then don't talk about it in front of us.

After all, your teen doesn't discuss things in front of you he doesn't want you to know. So the next time you start a conversation around your teen, and he asks, "Wait, what happened?" remember that saying, "Nothing. Forget about it," doesn't quite cut it.

When Teasing Your Teen Becomes Hurtful

Part of personal privacy is respecting your teen as a person and knowing the boundaries you shouldn't cross. All parents poke fun at their teens, just like teens poke fun at their parents. But just like with anything, if you don't respect or even notice what the boundaries are, joking can go too far and become hurtful or offensive. All of a sudden you're getting the silent treatment, or your teen is crying instead of laughing when you thought you were just saying the same things you'd been saying for years. So, here are some situations and some tips for making sure you don't take a little fun too far.

"IF YOU SAY THAT *ONE* MORE TIME . . ."

Meg is fourteen years old, and she's learning how to play the violin. She has only been playing for a year and she knows that she's not that good, but she enjoys it and feels like she's improving. When she practices, her father, Harry, often jokes with her about how she squeaks and creaks. Meg laughs along with Harry because she knows she does squeak quite a bit, but after all the jokes Harry's cracked, it's hard for Meg to keep laughing.

It's a Saturday afternoon and Meg is practicing violin in her bedroom with the door shut. Her father comes in, which makes her a little nervous because she doesn't want to sound bad in front of him.

"Don't mind me, Meg. I just need to borrow some computer paper."

"Okay," Meg says as she pretends to fiddle with her music so she won't have to play until her dad leaves.

"Just continue like I'm not even here. I'll be out in a minute."

Meg begins to play.

"Gotta reoil those strings, huh, Meg?" Harry chuckles.

"Whatever, Dad."

"It's like a car coming to a short stop . . . *screeeech*." Harry gives Meg a playful nudge.

"Could you be a bigger jerk right now?"

"Excuse me? What did you just call me?"

"A jerk." Meg looks him right in the eye, without any shame.

"You're totally out of line, Megan. I don't know where you get off calling me a jerk, but you better re-think your behavior and clean up that language. You're being completely disrespectful."

"*Me!* What about you? It's amazing. He can't even see what he's doing . . ." Meg continues, then mutters under her breath.

"What am I doing that I don't see? You can talk to me if you have a question, you don't need to mutter un-der your breath."

"You really want to know?"

"Yeah."

"Okay. You make me feel like crap when you make fun of my playing. Is that a good enough response for you? Now would you please get out of my room?"

"Are you serious? I never realized—"

"Would you *please* get out?"

"No, we need to talk about this."

"*No!* We don't! You need to get out of here!"

Because Harry came in and told Meg to go ahead and play, even though she had chosen to stop while he was there, it seems to Meg like he tricked her into trusting him. He told her that he wanted her to be comfortable, and then he made fun of her right off the bat. Now Meg thinks Harry only wanted her to play so he'd have an excuse to make fun of her. That doesn't do anything for her self-esteem, and it's what made this time worse than any other.

So he got her to tell him what was wrong and now he wants to talk about it—well, *that's* not going to work. Harry should have left the room after Meg said what was bothering her and made it clear she didn't want to talk about it. Right now, she is upset and doesn't want to get into the details, so the best thing for Harry to do would be to leave when Meg asks him to, and then come back later and talk about it when she's cooled down. Then both Meg and Harry would have a better chance of staying civil and actually having a productive conversation, rather than getting into a screaming match in which both of them are defensive and misunderstand what the other is saying.

In a case like this, where a teen keeps it to herself, it's going to be hard to know that a problem even exists before she actually blows up at you. The only way to make that situation any better is to change your response when she calls you names or yells at you. To prevent it from getting that far, though, you'll have to figure out if jokes you're making are bugging your teen, and that'll be hard because teens don't like to let you know you're getting to them. So, besides having a better attitude when you *do* find out something's wrong, the best thing for you to do is try to be more sensitive.

If you catch yourself poking fun and notice a hint of unease in your teen, or even notice that you're just not getting a good response, you need to stop and ask yourself if you're going too far. In fact, you might even want to stop every once in a while and ask your teen, "You don't mind if I say these things, do you? You know I'm only kidding with you, right?" You'll get a straightforward response if you let your teen understand that whatever he says is okay because you actually want to know the truth.

Just remember, it's not always easy for teens to tell their parents that something is bothering them, especially if they don't want to make you feel bad. Asking is good, but being aware of how your teen is responding *all the time* is even better.

A FOLLOW-UP CONVERSATION: "WE NEED TO TALK; I NEED TO APOLOGIZE."

Later that night, Meg is watching TV in the living room when Harry comes in to apologize for what he said earlier that day.

"Can we talk?" Harry sits down on the couch.

"You obviously can. You've got a big mouth."

"I understand you're mad, but you need to realize I didn't mean to hurt you. I thought I was being funny and joking around. I never meant to insult you or your playing or your effort."

Meg returns this apology with silence, as she switches channels rapidly.

"Look, I understand you're hurt and that's the last thing I would ever want. I spend my life trying to keep you from getting hurt, so you can imagine how awful I feel. But I know I'm not the one who got hurt here. I just want to say I'm sorry, and in the future I'll try not to say stupid things like that anymore. Okay?"

"Whatever. I don't care."

You can have this type of follow-up talk in any situation, really. It doesn't have to be in the same day; it could be the next morning or even later. What's key is that your teen is listening and willing to talk. If you go into her room and she won't even look at you, you might want to wait and try again after more time has passed. The time may never seem right—she may never start the conversation by looking at you and pouring out her feelings—but eventually you'll just have to talk and hope for the best.

Even if your teen doesn't respond, it's important that you say something, because she will probably hear you whether or not she accepts your apology or says she understands. Basically, don't expect it to be like the conversations parents have with their kids at the end of sitcoms. Your teen will probably hear you, but there won't be any sappy music, and probably no big hugs and smiles.

One thing you also want to avoid is making it seem as if you're the one who deserves pity. Just because you feel awful that you did something, it doesn't mean she should feel bad for you. So, when Harry says, "I spend my life trying to keep you from getting hurt, so you can imagine how awful I feel," he almost blows it, but fortunately he redeems himself with "But I know I'm not the one who got hurt here."

The Worst Kind of Teasing

Don't tease us about something we're the least bit insecure about—for example, how developed our body is compared to other teens' bodies.

Don't make fun of us in front of our friends. It makes us self-conscious. We may laugh along but it's almost always a cover. It's even worse to do this in front of a new friend or a boyfriend or girlfriend.

Don't run a joke into the ground. Say it once. It might be funny the first time, but the second time it probably isn't.

(Also, here's a hint: "switching channels rapidly" is a sign that she's listening, because she's not focused on what's going on in a particular show. Of course, that doesn't mean she isn't listening if she is watching something, but it will probably work out better if you save the talk for when she isn't watching her favorite show.)

That's Not Teen Spirit

"THAT'S SO RUDE."

Kevin is a thirteen-year-old eighth-grader. It's a Saturday afternoon and he and his father, Louis, have just come home from his baseball practice. Kevin is still in his sweaty uniform, having a bite to eat in the kitchen. Louis comes in and hands Kevin a three-pack of Old Spice deodorant.

"What's this?" Kevin asks, with a disgusted look.

"Deodorant. You can put two of the sticks away in the cabinet and give it a try."

"That's so rude, Dad."

"What did I do?"

"Why don't you just say 'you smell like crap'?"

"Hey! Kevin, that's not what I meant! I just thought you'd want to try some."

"Dad, I can decide this on my own. You don't have to insult me, okay?" Kevin storms out of the kitchen.

Although this will probably blow over in a day or two, and Kevin might even start using the deodorant, this is still a bad way to approach the situation. Louis shouldn't have taken it upon himself to buy deodorant for Kevin. He should have let Kevin decide when to use deodorant, and probably which kind. In this scenario Kevin is offended because he thinks Louis is saying something negative about him.

SUBTLETY, THE OTHER OPTION

Kevin and his father, Louis, are on their way home from baseball practice on a Saturday afternoon. Louis has something he's been wanting to talk to Kevin about.

"Kev, I have a question for you."

"What?"

"Do you use deodorant?"

"No . . . why? What are you saying?"

"Nothing. I just thought you might want to consider using it before practice, and in general. You know, to get in the habit."

"Are you trying to say I smell? 'Cause you're *not* being very subtle about it."

"I'm not saying that at all, Kevin. It's just a fact that as you get older, you sweat more. It was just a thought. I know that I hate being around people who smell, and I'm sure you do, too. Everyone needs to wear deodorant eventually. I figured if you start wearing it now and get used to it, it won't ever be an issue later."

"Okay. Whatever."

This conversation is great because Louis doesn't make it a big deal. It's not a pressing issue or a safety issue—it's really a "nothing" issue, so it's best to treat it that way. Louis approaches Kevin casually, and doesn't say anything negative about him.

He leaves it to Kevin to make the decision for himself, and never says he needs deodorant or should use it. It's good that Louis keeps it all casual and insignificant, because this can be a sensitive issue for some teens, and it could have been interpreted as insulting. Louis also made it impersonal by telling him that bodies change and that everyone needs to think about deodorant at some point. This way Kevin didn't need to feel insulted or attacked. Kevin probably concluded "My dad's just looking out for me."

On the completely opposite end of the spectrum, it's highly possible that your teen will be dying to use deodorant way before it's necessary. In that case, let him (or her, although with girls it's not usually an issue). It can't hurt, so if it makes him feel more mature or helps him fit in with his friends, let him pick some out and wear it whenever he pleases. It can only boost his confidence.

Snooping: A Lose-Lose Proposition

OR, YOU COULD HAVE JUST ASKED

Sally has just spoken to her friend Margot. The two women have teenage daughters in the same grade at school. Margot has just told Sally that her daughter, Marianne, has been studying and stressing out for an upcoming biology test in Ms. Howard's class. Sally's daughter also has Ms. Howard, but strangely enough, her daughter has not mentioned or shown any sign of having a test soon. Worried that her daughter is slacking off, Sally decides to take matters into her own hands.

First, to be sure that her daughter also has the test, Sally searches for her daughter's agenda in her backpack, only to find the previous bio test marked with the letter *D*. Furious that Dana didn't tell her about the grade, she takes out the test. She puts the agenda back in the bag, forgetting to check about the upcoming test. When Dana returns home from the movies, Sally greets her at the door. Already frustrated that Dana was choosing a movie over her grades, Sally hands Dana the test.

"What's this?" Dana asks rudely.

"You tell me."

Confused, Dana opens the folded papers, and to her surprise she sees that it is her old bio test.

"That's why I didn't show it to you yet. I knew you would react like this. Where did you get this, anyway?"

"In your backpack," Sally replies confidently.

"So now you are looking through all my personal stuff? Oh, but feel free! Why would *I* need any personal space anyway? I'm just a stupid teenager, right?"

"Your business is my business, especially when it comes to school. You are slacking off and I'm just looking out for you."

Not sure how to respond to her mother, Dana walks off. Feeling like her daughter doesn't respect her, Sally follows Dana into her room.

"By the way, Dana, you better start studying because I'm expecting an *A* from you on your test tomorrow."

"I don't have one, genius. Where did you come up with that one, anyway?"

"Don't lie to me, and get rid of that fresh mouth of yours! Marianne has Ms. Howard and she's been studying hard all week for the test tomorrow, *your* test. So, I suggest you get your act together."

"Marianne is in *regular* bio. I'm in intensive. So once again, no, I don't have a test tomorrow. Could you please leave *my* room now?"

A little embarrassed, Sally decides to back off the situation and leaves her daughter's room.

Some parents do not understand that the simplest thing, such as an agenda or date book, can be personal and private to a teenager. When Sally said she looked in Dana's backpack, Dana interpreted it as "I don't respect your privacy, therefore I don't respect you." Although it is better that Sally did not lie about looking through Dana's stuff, she should have known not to do it in the first place.

You are probably thinking, "Well, then, how would she ever know her child was failing tests? If she doesn't know, she can't help prevent it in the future." It's simple. *Just ask.* When parents *choose* to look through their teen's stuff, they are setting up a barrier between themselves and their teen. It's harder for a teen to confide in her parents about school or other things when she thinks her parents probably heard or read about it somewhere else first.

(Teens shouldn't feel the need to hide their grades from their parents, but sometimes they do. See chapter 2, "Just Accept It—I'm *Not* Going to Harvard," about academic pressure.)

TIP

Don't say things like "Your business is my business" or "Everything you do is my business." It makes teens feel like they have no space they can call their own.

Plus (believe it or not), not all things *are* parents' business.

Even if failing grades are involved, it just isn't a good idea to read your teenager's private things. Some of us like to write down everything in our notebooks and journals. Everybody knows that this helps teens deal with things, and we can't write freely if we think you're going to be snooping around and reading things that weren't meant for your eyes.

YOU'VE GOT MAIL . . . AND PROBLEMS

Anne's fourteen-year-old daughter, Ali, is "addicted" to the Internet. She is constantly sending e-mails and IM-ing (instant messaging) with her friends. Anne has always wondered what is being written in those e-mails and today is her chance to find out: Ali left her Internet mailbox open when she left for school that morning.

Anne decides to check the e-mail. She justifies it to herself by saying, "If Ali is going through something, it is my responsibility to find out what it is and help her with it." Anne starts to check the mail, and then the computer freezes.

If she leaves the computer like this, Ali will come home and see opened e-mails. Anne doesn't know Ali's password so she can't reboot and sign back in. The evidence is there. What is she going to do?

Anne decides to lie. When Ali gets home she tells her that she saw her computer was on this morning, and as a favor, since she's a nice mother, she turned it off for her. Ali mumbles a "thanks" and walks away.

Later that night, Ali gets back online. After she checks her e-mail, a friend IMs her and writes, "Ali, you get my e-mail? Doesn't it sound like a good idea?" Ali has no idea what e-mail her friend is referring to because there weren't any new e-mails in her in-box. She looks at her already-viewed mail and there it is.

Ali's first reaction is "I was probably tired and forgot about reading it." She decides to check, though, just to make sure she isn't crazy, and looks at the status line for the e-mail. It reads "Last viewed at 9:35 a.m.," *after* she left for school. Jumping to a reasonable conclusion, Ali storms downstairs and confronts her mother.

"How dare you read my e-mails? Who the hell do you think you are? That is my private business, not yours!" Ali screams at the top of her lungs.

"Calm down. I already told you, I did you a favor and shut down your computer, that's all. That's the only thing I did."

"Do you think I'm stupid? Why are you lying to me? Somebody was reading my mail at 9:35 a.m., and it wasn't me and it wasn't the dog, so I know it was you! You've been invading my privacy again, and this time I have evidence!"

"Okay, you're right. I lied. But the only reason I read your e-mail was to protect you and make sure that everything was going okay. You barely talk to me about anything anymore, so I wanted to check up."

Not surprisingly, this doesn't make Ali feel better.

"Aren't you even going to admit you did something wrong? Stop justifying yourself and at least apologize. You violated my privacy. Don't think I'm ever going to tell you anything ever again!" Ali shrieks as she storms up to her room and violently slams the door.

Some parents don't understand why it's a big deal to teens if parents read their e-mail. Well, think of e-mail as a diary, but even more personal than that. The teen sees your reading her e-mail as a violation of her space, and it is, even if it is virtual space. But these are the exchanges she has with her friends, so it's not just an invasion of *her* personal privacy, it's her friends' privacy as well.

When Anne says, "I just wanted to make sure everything was okay," Ali hears, "I'm just making an excuse for doing something completely inappropriate. I don't want to admit that I was wrong."

Don't make your teenager feel like she needs to assume the parent role and tell you to apologize or recognize what's wrong. If anything, we recommend you fess up right away and set an example by being completely honest with your teen. If not, you can't expect her to be honest with you.

If Anne had been smart, she would have been honest from the start.

A BETTER APPROACH

"How dare you read my e-mails? Who the hell do you think you are? That is my private business, not yours!" Ali screams at the top of her lungs.

"You're right. I shouldn't have read your e-mail. I am really sorry. You never tell me anything anymore, and I did it because I was concerned about you, but that's no excuse. It was a mistake, and I apologize."

"What made you think I wouldn't catch you? Do you take me for an idiot? Do you think you're setting a good example for me by snooping around and being a liar?"

"No, I don't think you are an idiot, and honestly, I'm glad you caught me, because I needed to learn a lesson. I shouldn't have lied in the first place," Anne says calmly.

Ali storms off.

The reason Ali walked away from this situation is because there is nothing left for her to say. Anne gave in on every point, and there's nothing for Ali to attack anymore. Anne has apologized and admitted to the wrongdoing.

Anne shouldn't be expecting Ali to just say, "Okay, Mom, no big deal. I love you," because it doesn't work like that. In a situation like this, you should expect your teen to storm off and be angry about it for a few days. You have just violated her space. In your house, e-mail and the other things she writes are one of the few places where she can really feel personal ownership. It's a very serious thing to take away.

In both the scenarios above, Anne says her motive was that Ali doesn't tell her about her life anymore, but there's a big difference between them. In the first scenario, Anne uses it as an excuse to justify her actions and to ask for sympathy. Not surprisingly, the whole conversation is tainted in Ali's eyes; what she hears is "You never tell me anything, so it's not my fault, it's yours." In the second scenario, she explains herself with the same motive, but she admits that what she did was wrong. Ali probably believes that's why her mother went snooping around, but she will never think it is justified. Trying to justify it will just make her angrier. Without an apology, the explanation doesn't help you.

Also, remember that if you decide to admit that you were wrong, then you really shouldn't plan on doing it again. The next time you get caught, there may not be a large explosion, but your teen might just pretend that you don't exist, and it might last for quite a while.

When it comes to e-mail, Ali is a lot more advanced than Anne, and even if Anne thinks she has covered her tracks well, chances are she hasn't. If Anne doesn't tell Ali what she did before she finds out on her own, things can only get worse. So if you somehow find yourself in this situation, here's the best thing you can do.

THE BEST APPROACH

Anne decides that she'd better be honest, because she knows that Ali will probably figure out that she looked at her e-mail. When Ali gets home, Anne decides to take the opportunity to tell Ali what she did and why she did it before she finds out for herself.

"Ali, I have something to tell you, and I want you to just hear me out, okay? Let me finish talking, and then you can respond, okay?"

"Yeah, okay. What?"

"Well, earlier today, I went to clean your room and I saw that your computer was left on. Lately we haven't been communicating as much, and you're always glued to your computer screen, so I made a really bad decision and looked at your e-mail. I only read one. That was it. I shouldn't have read even that one, but I did, and I'm really sorry. I just wanted you to know that I know what I did was wrong, and I'm sorry. I know that I'll have to earn back your trust, so I just hope you let me do that."

Ali will do one of two things at this point. She will walk away because she is too dumbfounded and disappointed to do anything else, or she will scream at the top of her lungs all the reasons why she shouldn't tell you anything (see above).

Either way, what's done is done. But in this scenario, Anne plays her cards well. She doesn't praise herself for being honest, because it shouldn't have happened in the first place, and Ali will not be shy about pointing that out. She shows Ali that she knows what she did was wrong, and now she can make sure she doesn't do it again.

One final note on e-mails and IMs: try not to lean over our shoulders when we're typing to our friends online. It's a violation of privacy, just like reading our e-mail, and it's also really obnoxious.

Chapter 2

"Just Accept It— I'm *Not* Going to Harvard":

Surviving High School with Your Teen

Parents often assume that the first year in high school is the transition year, the only time when it is "reasonable" for teens to be struggling as they get adjusted to the workload, the social scene and the extracurricular activities. What parents can sometimes overlook is that each year of high school presents new challenges, whether we're taking SATs or finding a date to the prom, and sometimes the old ones don't really go away, either.

Just as much as helping your teens do their best, your goal as a parent should be to ease these pressures and worries. Having a parent who is not supportive during all of the transitions of the high school years can put unnecessary and damaging stress on teens.

We have been through this, and we know from talking to our friends the best and worst ways to handle the different pressures your teen is facing. In this chapter, we will take you all the way from how to help your teen cope with bad grades in bio to how not to say the one thing that guarantees he won't go to the college of your choice.

Apples and Oranges, and the Grapevine

In chapter 1, the topic of snooping was addressed in the story of Sally and her daughter, Dana. Another issue besides personal privacy that surfaced in this conversation was talking to other parents about your child.

It's one thing when teenagers encounter competition among their peers at school—they know this comes with the territory—but when they feel they can't escape competition because it's a component of life at home, their self-confidence is at stake. When parents talk to other parents and compare their teenagers' progress, it feels like competition to teens. A lot of the time, parents don't realize teens think they are being compared, but when you simply ask, "Is Johnny in the advanced math class?" it puts an unspoken pressure on the teenagers.

Below you'll find Sally and Dana having the same conversation as they did before, but this time it goes in a different direction.

"YOU TALKED TO HER MOM ABOUT ME? TRAITOR!"

Sally has just spoken to her friend Margot. The two women have teenage daughters in the same grade at school. Margot has just told Sally that her daughter, Marianne, has been studying and stressing out for an upcoming biology test in Ms. Howard's class. Sally's daughter also has Ms. Howard, but strangely enough, her daughter has not mentioned or shown any sign of having a test soon. Worried that her daughter is slacking off, Sally decides to take matters into her own hands.

First, to be sure that her daughter also has the test, Sally searches for her daughter's agenda in her backpack, only to find the previous bio test, marked with the letter *D*. Furious that Dana didn't tell her about the grade, she takes out the test. She puts the agenda back in the bag, forgetting to check about the upcoming test. When Dana returns home from the movies, Sally greets her at the door. Already frustrated that Dana was choosing a movie over her grades, Sally hands Dana the test.

"What's this?" asks Dana, rudely.

"You tell me. And while you're at it, why don't you tell me why I never saw it."

Confused, Dana opens the folded papers, and to her surprise she sees that it is her old bio test.

"This is *exactly* why I didn't show it to you yet. I knew you would react like this. Where did you get this anyway?"

"In your backpack," Sally replies confidently.

"So now you are looking through all my personal stuff? Oh, but feel free! Why would *I* need any personal space anyway? I'm just a stupid teenager, right?"

"Your business is my business, especially when it comes to school. You are slacking off instead of studying for your test tomorrow."

"I don't have one, genius."

"Don't lie to me! Margot told me that Marianne has been studying hard all week for the test tomorrow. So, I suggest you get your act together."

"Marianne is in *regular* bio. I'm in intensive."

A little embarrassed, Sally decides to back off from the situation and leave her daughter's room.

Unfortunately, Dana isn't done talking about it. "I can't believe you were talking about me behind my back. *If you want me to do well in intensive, then stop making this a competition between you and your pathetic friend Margot.* This is about *me*, not you and *not* her."

We know Dana is angry because her mother went into her backpack and she's embarrassed by her bad grade, but why is she so hurt that Sally is talking to other parents?

Teenagers perceive your casual conversations with other parents as opportunities to compare their accomplishments and brag. When a teenager receives a bad grade she worries that the entire parent network will know about it. At a time like this, teenagers are always thinking about how others perceive them, whether it's their parents, other parents, or their peers.

Dana got so upset because she felt like her mother didn't trust her, and more importantly, she didn't want to be compared to Marianne. She was probably thinking, "If she trusted me then she wouldn't feel the need to ask my friends' parents about my life."

Dana knows that she should have told her parents about the D on the last bio test, but maybe she wasn't ready to approach them. She might have needed time to meet with the teacher to discuss how she could make up the grade before she felt confident enough about herself to tell them.

You're probably thinking, "We should be the easiest people to tell," but the truth is, for a teenager, you are the hardest people to explain grades and other stuff to. We value your opinion so much that we can't bear to see your face as we disappoint you with another bad grade. You can help by letting your teen know that you aren't there to judge, you are there to help. You can only achieve this by communicating *with* her, instead of around her.

All teenagers know that it is impossible to avoid the topic of "How is your kid doing?" with other parents, but they also need to know that you are *just* talking, not looking for dirt or gossiping. Your teenager needs to understand that there is a difference between talking about her life and investigating it, and that you know what it is. Trust is key here.

The following scenes show different approaches we feel teens would be more receptive to.

AGAIN, ASKING IS ALWAYS GOOD

Margot has just told Sally that Marianne has been stressing out studying for an upcoming biology test in Ms. Howard's class. Worried that her daughter is slacking off, Sally decides to ask Dana directly. After all, Marianne and Dana are two different people, with two different methods of studying.

"How was school?"

"Okay."

"Have any tests?"

"No . . . why?"

"Just curious. I was talking to Margot today and she mentioned that Marianne is having a hard time managing her school work. So I just wanted to make sure you're doing all right."

"Yep, I'm fine. Marianne just exaggerates so when she does badly she can blame it on all the stress."

"She said Ms. Howard was giving a really hard bio test. Do you have the same one?"

"Nope."

"All right. Are you finding her class a challenge also?"

"Yeah, actually . . . I'm struggling a lot. I'm gonna go try and meet with her next week."

"Good idea. It looks like you got stuck with my genes! Maybe Dad can help you out if you want. Science was always his thing. Anyway, if there's anything I can help you with, just let me know."

This is an example of successful communication between parent and child. Because Sally approached Dana with an encouraging attitude and an open mind, Dana was receptive. Sally wasn't making accusations, like in the conversation in chapter 1. Because her mother told her she wanted to make sure Dana was all right, Dana was open to sharing her struggle; she felt her mother would be helpful, not critical. When Sally says, "I just wanted to make sure you're doing all right," Dana hears, "I care about you" instead of "Why can't you be more on top of your work like Marianne?"

In addition, if you tell your kid it's happened to you, like Sally did, then your teen will feel a burden lifted off her back and you will have a mutual understanding. This is a good way to connect with your kids and make them feel comfortable sharing information.

A good way to check and see if your teen benefited from this conversation is to have a follow-up conversation in a week. (But remember to wait a week. If you keep asking over and over again, they will hear, "I don't trust you to stay on top of your work, and therefore I need to keep reminding you.") This follow-up conversation can be very direct if you tried the approach above and it worked for you. You can ask very bluntly how the meeting with the teacher went, etc.

Remember, though, that you may think the conversation went well when in reality it didn't; Dana may have understood the message that Sally was trying to send but *your* teen might not. Every teen responds differently, so things won't always run as smoothly as they did for Dana and Sally. For instance, your teen may get defensive when you say, "Are you finding her class a challenge also?" She may respond sharply, with something like "Why? Because I'm so stupid?"

You know your teenager, so if you really think she will start attacking you if you take a direct approach, try a more indirect conversation. For kids who have trouble picking up underlying messages it probably wouldn't be the best approach, but if defensiveness is a problem, this could be what works for you.

SUBTLETY CAN BE NICE, TOO

Sally has just spoken to her friend Margot. Worried that her daughter is slacking off, Sally decides to tell Dana directly that she spoke with Margot, and wants to make sure that she is doing okay in the class. She knows that Dana has not been a strong science student in the past and may be embarrassed because of it. Sally has decided she won't put Dana on the spot, she'll just mention it in passing.

"I was talking to Margot today because we were making plans for Marianne's birthday. She mentioned that it would be a nice release to go out to dinner because Marianne has been really stressed out by her bio class. Can you do Friday night? I don't want to interfere if you've already made plans to go out with friends or study."

"Yeah, I can do Friday."

"Good. I hope you know that if you need any help
managing school and stuff, we're always here for you. It
sounds like a lot of kids are having trouble with classes,
and we know from experience how impossible high
school can be. So if you want any tricks from the old
bag or just need to take a break, let me know."

"Thanks, Mom . . . ," Dana says as she smiles and
walks off.

There is a lot of power in casual conversation. The trick is
to keep it short and sweet, so your child will absorb the message instead of being bored by it—she will be more likely to
follow through on your offer to help. Try not to get frustrated
if your teen doesn't respond immediately. Sometimes it takes
us a little while to absorb what you're trying to tell us.

Another thing to keep in mind: you might state everything perfectly, but your teen's mind could be focused somewhere else. That's a problem with us teenagers; we live in a
bubble and sometimes it's hard to get us focused on something that doesn't interest us. You think you're getting your
message across because we're nodding our heads, but we
might just be hearing "Blah blah blah." If you think this is the
case with your teenager, then you may want to have a follow-
up conversation in a week or two and casually ask how her
work's going. This will help you confirm if your child is receptive to an indirect method like this.

"LET ME GUESS. MARIANNE IS A BETTER DAUGHTER THAN I AM?"

Recently, Dana's academic performance has been
weak, and her mother is concerned. Dana is struggling
to maintain her grades and Sally fears that she isn't even

What you say	What we hear
"We have dinner Friday night with the Smiths."	"I don't really care what you may have planned and I don't respect you enough to check with you before making plans."
"Can you do Friday night? I don't want to interfere if you've already made plans to go out with friends or study."	"I understand you have a life outside of this family, so I wanted to respect you by checking with you before making any plans."

This may sound extreme but we feel like we should be included in these decisions, even if we don't have that much of an influence.

trying to keep up with the course load. When Margot mentions that Marianne said Dana is slacking off in class, Sally decides to say something to Dana.

"How was school?"

"It's school. How good could it be?"

"That's true. Although I did enjoy going to some classes back in the old days."

"Like what? P.E.?"

"No, like math . . . I hated science though. Isn't

there even one class or one teacher you like in the slightest?"

"I kind of like history. Depends on the teacher. Bio's gonna be the death of me though. I hate it more than anything."

"Yeah, so I've heard."

"What the hell does that mean?"

"Well, I was talking to Margot today and—"

"Of course you were. You're always talking to Margot. Let me guess. She thinks I'm not as good as Marianne. Well, she's right. Her daughter's perfect and I'm not. I don't get A's on my tests, but you know what? At least I'm not boring like she is. At least I don't lie to make other people think I'm great!"

"Dana, I never said any of that. Please stop assuming things. What I was going to say is, I spoke to Margot today and supposedly Marianne said that a lot of kids have been struggling with their work lately. I just wanted to make sure that you feel comfortable with everything."

"I'm fine. Are we done here?"

"No . . . you just screamed at me and I hadn't even made my point yet. Why were you so resentful when I mentioned Margot's name? Why would I be mad if you weren't getting straight A's?"

"I don't know. Go away."

"Dana, this problem isn't going to go away. We'll talk about it later."

"Uch."

Okay, first things first: a comment like "So I've heard" doesn't fly very high with a short-fused teenager (which happens to be every teenager, you might have noticed). What your teen hears when you say, "So I've heard" is something more like "Everyone who's anyone knows about this. Everyone knows how *dumb* you are." But even though parents should try to avoid making a comment like this—and that's what might have been responsible for triggering this *particular* fight—Dana would probably have blown up sometime soon anyway. This issue of competition with Marianne has obviously been brewing inside of Dana for a long time.

Actually, Sally handled the situation very well; she was calm and considerate before *and* after Dana had her sudden outburst, which is much more important than the fact that Sally was responsible for the outburst. Dana, or any teen, will be sensitive when the subject of grades comes up, and the chances are high that the outburst would have happened anyway. The main thing here is how you handle the outburst, because no matter what you say it's going to happen eventually, especially at a time when they're feeling more anxiety than usual about the subject.

This conversation may sound like one you don't want to have, but the truth is, the first step with a teenager is getting them to blurt out their real issues. The only way you'll find out a teenager's true feelings about an issue is when they are upset about it and really pissed off. Trust us on this.

The sample conversation above was about grades, but Dana might just as easily be giving Sally a hard time about what's for dinner, when the real problem is that she feels like she is competing against Marianne. Until they really get into a fight, Sally won't ever find out that it's not just about the lame meat loaf.

Once the real root of the problem has come out, letting your teen cool off is really important. Sally didn't let the situation head in a bad direction. She allowed Dana to vent and then gave her time to cool off. Sally knew that this outburst was bound to happen, and she rightfully pointed out that it was Dana who made the assumptions. This was a good way to end the conversation because it left the ball in the parent's court, but let the teen have the last word, which is something we value tremendously.

If your instincts are telling you that your teen is not the type of person to abandon her obligations as a student, then trust your instincts, at least to start.

In this situation, Marianne really might be trying to make Dana look bad to both her mom and to Sally. It may sound shocking that we could make such a suggestion, but we know firsthand that some teenagers can get so desperate to impress their parents and others that they put a bad light on another friend to make themselves look better. You need to find out if that's what is going on. If you are sure that this isn't the case, you can skip this follow-up conversation.

"Dana, earlier I think you said Marianne lies to make people think better of her. What exactly did you mean by that?"

"What do you think I meant? I meant what I said— Marianne cares what other people think and I don't. She tries to impress Margot with her grades and she thinks she gets bonus points for doing better on a test than someone like me. She probably lies and tells her mother that I do badly so she can look like the better student. And it looks like you fell for that bull too."

"It's true. I did hear from Margot that kids were struggling with bio. And that's why I wanted to talk to *you*, and not Marianne or Margot. I wanted to make sure that you were doing okay. I wanted to make sure that you knew we're here for you. I wanted to make sure that I got the facts from you because I trust you with your work and I trust that you will come to me or to the teacher if there is a problem."

Dana gives Sally a blank stare.

"Now can we start this conversation over again?" asks Sally in a calm voice.

"Fine."

"You said bio was hard this year. Tell me about it. . . ."

Your teens will be more willing to open up when they feel like you have confidence in them and their ability to do well. Most of you are probably thinking that in reality this approach would be too simple and wouldn't work for you and your teen. If you set the conversation up with the right tone, though, like Sally did, then you are guaranteed productive results. Dana was obviously bursting to tell Sally about Marianne and her warped ways of impressing her mother; all you need to do is ask and let your teen take it from there.

Maybe your teen really is slacking off, though. It could be because she feels she could never get an A in the class, so why even try? Also, if she was having trouble in a class, she probably kept it from you because she was ashamed, or didn't want to let you down. Teens are constantly seeking their parents' approval; therefore, it's really hard for them to open up about a struggle they are experiencing. At this point, the only way they will open up is if you bluntly state to them, "It's not about the grade."

"WHO CARES ABOUT BIO, ANYWAY?"

"Dana, I think we need to start this conversation over again."

"I have nothing to say."

"Well, you blew up at me earlier when I asked how things were going. I really want to know why it upsets you so much when we talk about your work and progress."

"Because you care more about this crap than I do."

"I care because it's my job to care. I want to see you succeed and enjoy the things you engage in."

"Well, I don't care about school or grades, so stop trying to make me care. It's not going to happen. Now please remove yourself from my room so I can pretend to do my homework."

"I'm not finished with this conversation, Dana. You can't expect me to just accept that as an answer. I want to know why you hate school so much, and more importantly I want you to understand that I don't care about your academic scores as long as you try. The letter grade isn't the important part if you're really making an effort."

"Well, I have no interest in trying in a subject like bio. It's not like I want to be a doctor or anything. Now go away."

At this point, you may want to try to relate to her, to let her know you've been there, but your teen's response may still be "Good, now bug off." If you know she could get better grades if she tried, the only thing you can really do is calmly explain the importance of doing your best in school, and try not to sound too preachy. One way you could say it is like this:

"I know you don't want to listen to me say this again and again, but hear me out one last time. As much as grades aren't important to *us*, we know that one day soon they may be important to you. We don't want you to look back and regret that you didn't try harder in bio because your grades are keeping you out of the college or profession of *your* choice. We just want the best for you, and therefore we push you to strive harder, but we are always one hundred percent behind you. Even if you don't do well, there is something to learn from trying hard, and that will stay with you forever. Persistence is what will let you achieve the dreams of your choice."

They may be obnoxious to you when you say this, and respond with "Okay, cheeseball," but that's probably because they know you're right and don't want to admit it. After all, no teen wants to give her parents the satisfaction of being right. It would be too nice of us.

If your teens are practically failing their courses, and receiving academic warnings, then you may want to take a more radical approach. First we suggest that you try the ap-

---

TIP

You might want to know that we do appreciate it when you recognize that we might not want to hear what you're saying ("I know you don't want to listen to me say this again and again, but hear me out one last time"); after all, we already know everything and we don't need to hear you tell us again. So prefacing a conversation that way can never hurt, because you're almost acknowledging that you understand we are experts too.

proach above, but if that doesn't work, you may want to give them an incentive to work.

When we say incentive, we don't mean you should bribe them to work, like offering them a car if they get straight As. Bribery is not a good approach because it will teach your teenagers bad values. Eventually your teen will start to take advantage of your bribes. It becomes too easy to turn it around and say something like "If you buy me a car, then I'll do my college applications." Also, teens really don't appreciate being bribed. It makes us feel like five-year-olds.

But you can still give your teen an incentive to do his work without making it bribery. You might want to take a privilege away until you see them make an *effort*.

When we say take a privilege away, we don't mean cold turkey, one hundred percent. For example, taking away all TV will just result in them being angry and rebelling against you—that is, not doing *any* of their work and adding to the frustration by not talking to you. Instead you could limit their TV/video game/IM privileges to something like an hour a night on weekdays. Once you see them begin to improve, you can slowly return these privileges to them and hope that by this time they understand the importance of trying. You can also tell them that if they don't keep up their efforts, the consequences will be harsher the next time.

One last thing: if it happens that Dana isn't struggling or slacking off, and Marianne is just a better student, the only thing Sally can do is accept it. If your teen is in this situation and accepts it, you need to also. If your teen is unhappy about it, urge her to focus on the things she is good at. Don't encourage her to look for things that she is better at than Marianne. You don't want to fuel her competitive side.

There's no set way to get your child to focus or to recognize the connection between getting good grades and achieving her goals. It all depends on the particular teenager. For example, if all your teen talks about is wanting to go to Harvard but her grades aren't great, she needs to understand that you can't do her work for her and you can't wave a wand to get her in.

YOU KNOW THEY CHECK YOUR TRANSCRIPT, RIGHT?

Recently, Jill's academic performance has been weak, and her father, Joel, is concerned. Jill is struggling to maintain her grades and Joel fears that she isn't even trying to keep up with the course load.

Joel worries because although Jill has really high goals for herself, like going to Harvard, with as little effort as Jill's been putting in, she will never achieve these goals.

"Jill, I know you have really awesome and ambitious goals for yourself. I think it's really great, and if you put the right amount of work into it I think it's possible for you to achieve those goals."

"Okay, thanks, Dad. . . ."

"But I'm worried, Jill. I don't think you're putting in the effort you need to if you really want to reach these goals. It's not like these are my goals for you. I want to help you achieve your own goals, and I think we both have to come to terms with how hard it is to get into a school like Harvard. I've watched people go through the college process and it's pretty gruesome. I don't want you to look back and regret that you didn't try as hard as you could in bio when a grade keeps you out of the college of *your* choice."

"So you think I'm slacking?"

"Well, I think it's important for us all to be clear on what a school like Harvard expects from its students and what they look for in applicants. If you're comfortable with the effort you're putting in and happy with the grades you're getting, then I am too. But if you feel like you're having trouble concentrating, or understanding something, and you could do better with some help, then I'd be more than happy to work with you to change that."

"Okay, I'll think about it. Thanks."

TIPS

- Be as straightforward as you can with your teen. We are more responsive when we know what the real issue is, or when everything's out in the open.
- When teens are struggling with something, try to relate their struggles to an experience you've had. It takes the pressure off of them and makes them realize they aren't the only ones who ever found themselves in a situation like the one they're in.
- It's good for teens to dream, and you should encourage them to strive to achieve their dreams, but part of your job is to make sure their feet stay on the ground. It's tricky, because you don't want to say, "Don't have dreams," or make them feel like you think they're not good enough to achieve them, but you should help them figure out which ones really are just dreams, and how to make the other ones a reality.

Even if you think she's never going to get into Harvard anyway, you've done everything you can to let her know that Harvard expects more than she's doing. Now the responsibility is in her hands and it's time for you to step back and try your best to be supportive through the process with each decision she makes. You can try to help her, but it's her life, and at a certain point if you become too involved in the process she will end up resenting you for it.

You've done the best you could, and if she doesn't get into Harvard because she didn't try her hardest, it will be a lesson for her that putting in effort does make a difference. You don't have to say "I told you so." In fact, it's better if you don't. She'll understand it herself; you can just help her get through a difficult time.

When It's Time for Time Management

We know that sometimes you think that if we would just manage things more sensibly, the way you want us to, there wouldn't be problems with grades.

It's true, teenagers love to waste time, and more importantly we love to procrastinate with our homework. As a parent, your instincts are probably telling you that it's your job to help them take control of the time-management situation. News flash: this isn't going to work.

The only way your teenagers will learn is the hard way, by screwing up and paying for the consequences. If you "butt into" their homework situation, all they will do is snap at you and see your worries as a challenge to their independence. They will just push you away to prove that they can manage their own time.

It's probably very frustrating to you, because if your teen just did what you said, you know he wouldn't have to go through that learning process. When he finds himself in a tight spot and asks you to help by writing a note excusing him from a test or to get an extension on an assignment, it might be tempting to do it because you feel sorry for him.

Well, don't. We're never going to learn if we don't suffer the consequences.

Instead, make suggestions and rules that will help your child learn to manage his time. Hopefully, if you do that, by the time he is in his late teens he will be able to handle all of his responsibilities without you stepping in and taking charge. Soon, he'll be in college, and he'll have to do it himself, so he might as well learn now—unless you're planning to go with him.

TV OR NOT TV—IS THAT THE QUESTION?

Angela is fed up with Bobby and his work ethic, so she decides it's time to have a talk with him. He wastes hours watching television when he could be spending all that time being productive and learning more. Angela figures that if she can just get Bobby interested in something else, he will stop watching TV as much as he does. She knows it won't be easy, so her logic leads her to this conclusion: if I tell him he can't watch TV until his homework is done, then he will get absorbed in his homework and won't watch TV as much. Nice thought, but, sorry.

Bobby is in the living room watching TV before dinner when Angela comes into the room.

"Bobby, we need to have a talk about watching TV," Angela says.

"What? I turn it on and I watch it. Great talking with you. 'Bye," Bobby says, and turns back to the TV.

Angela picks up the remote and shuts off the TV.

"I can't believe you did that!" Bobby says, outraged.

"I'm serious, Bobby. You spend all day just watching crap on TV when you could be studying and getting better grades in history."

"You don't know anything. It's not crap."

"That's not the point. From now on I want you to do all your homework and studying before you turn on the TV."

"That's *so* unfair!"

"No, it's not, and someday you'll thank me for doing this."

"Yeah, right."

"Now what homework do you have for tonight?"

Homework and Television

Suggest he choose one show a night to watch, and record the rest to watch over the weekend.

Suggest he take breaks from homework to fit in his favorite shows.

If all his favorite shows are on Thursday night and he doesn't want to tape them, suggest he arrange his homework schedule so that he can be ahead by then and watch his Thursday evening shows without any stress.

Bobby thinks, *"This one's easy."* He smiles at his
mom. "I don't have any homework," he says.

Let it be known that this will not work. If you say to your
teenager, "You can't watch TV until your homework is done,"
he will lie and say his homework is done when his favorite TV
show is on, or he will speed through his homework to get to
watch TV. It's a lose-lose situation. So what do you do? You
don't. In the homework arena, the only way a teenager is going to learn is by screwing up on his own. Once he fails, *then*
it's your turn to jump in and say, "Hey, I have a plan to take
action so that you can watch TV *and* do your homework."

Now that he's screwed up—which he probably won't admit even though it's written in bold on his test—he will be
looking for a solution. So here's your chance. Don't blow it.
There are a few things you can propose, but they'll only work
if you propose them properly.

So what is the proper way to present these ideas? Once
again, you can't expect your teenager to follow your suggestions immediately. It may take him a few more academic set-
backs to make it really click in his head that he needs to take
another approach. Also, we recommend that you present these
as suggestions, or options, instead of rules. If you make a no-
TV rule, he might not be watching TV when you knock on his
bedroom door, but that doesn't mean that homework is being
done. Nothing good can come out of a situation like that.

Instead, try an approach like this:

"I'm really sorry to hear about your test," Angela says.
Bobby gives her a blank stare and thinks, "Gee,
thanks for the sympathy. Here comes the lecture."
"I just wanted to tell you that when I was a teenager
it took me a while to figure out how to manage my

time. Honestly, I'm still not very good at it but I've learned a few things."

"Big deal," Bobby says, dismissively.

"Well, it doesn't have to be a big deal, but I know how much you like watching TV, and I know that you also want to do well in school. So I thought of a few plans that might give you the best of both worlds."

"No, thanks, Mom. I'll figure it out."

"Just hear me out. They aren't so bad. . . ."

"Okay, but make it quick. There's something on I have to see."

"Well, it seems to me that you don't always have time to watch your favorite shows *and* do your homework, so I was thinking maybe you could tape some of the shows and watch them over the weekend. Or, we could figure out an agenda that organizes you enough that you won't have to do any work on Thursday nights and you can just kick back and relax. What do you say?"

"I'll think about it. Thanks."

"Anytime. That's what I'm here for."

This should work (especially for middle schoolers, which sets up good habits for high school). But remember to be patient. Even after that conversation, Bobby might not change his TV and homework habits. They say that old habits are hard to break. Well, new habits are hard to make, too. Wait a couple of weeks and see if your teen is doing any better at getting his homework and studying done. You'll know because if he's doing better, he'll be proud to tell you when you ask.

If things haven't changed, follow up by asking if he's sticking to any of the plans you discussed. Go over them and explain again that this approach will solve his homework problems. You might have to do this three or four times, but eventually you will see an improvement in your teenager's habits and grades.

"EXCUSE ME FROM ENGLISH CLASS JUST THIS ONCE AND I'LL LOVE YOU FOREVER!"

Alex has always been stressed out about homework because he doesn't plan out his work over an extended period of time and he ends up doing all the work at the last minute. Lately, he has been so tired pulling all-nighters to catch up that he hasn't been able to function as efficiently as he usually does. It's gotten to the point where his work isn't getting done on time, and he's desperate.

Alex is a junior, so every individual grade has a large effect on his term grades. For the second time this year he is desperate, so he decides to ask his mom, Susan, for a note excusing him from writing an essay. Susan is torn. She doesn't want to say no and have it hurt her child's chance at a better grade, but she knows that it would be a bad choice. She did this for him once before and she worries that if she keeps doing it he will never learn to manage his time and work, and when he gets to college, he will be lost.

"Mom, look at me. I'm dying here. I could really use your help. I haven't slept in four days, and if I don't get this note from you, it could destroy my chances of getting into Michigan, and that's my dream."

"Alex, I would love to give you this note, but you needed one the other week and I don't think it's right for you to ask me to do this again."

"You realize you are ruining my chance at a good grade, right?"

"That's not fair. We talked about this before. You
need to start planning ahead instead of leaving it for the
last second."

"Mom, I promise I'll stop doing it. After today, I'm
done with the all-nighters, and I'm done procrastinating.
I'll do whatever you want me to do. You were right and I
was wrong. But now I've learned my lesson, so *please*
help me out."

"It's not like this is the first time this has happened.
You always do this to yourself. You told me last time
you would change and you haven't. I'm sorry."

It's one thing if a teenager needs a note because something came up that wasn't his fault, such as illness, but it's another when the teenager leaves it to the last minute because
his backup plan is Mommy or Daddy.

It will probably be very hard for you to say no. But like
Alex, your child may have a study-habit problem that needs
fixing. If Alex could continue to rely on his mother to bail him
out, he might never even try to fix it. Susan needed to let him
fail so that he could finally learn that she won't always be
there to pick him up when he falls. If she had caved in in the
end and decided to write him the letter, then she would be letting him get away with it again and the cycle would continue.

"Do Something with Your Life": Struggling to Agree on Extracurricular Activities

Getting good grades isn't the only thing teens have to deal with. One of the biggest pressures teenagers encounter involves their extracurricular activities, or lack thereof. Teens see extracurricular activities as a way to get involved in their community while enjoying themselves or simply to get away from the pressures of academics and/or social problems. Unfortunately, parents don't always see extracurriculars the same way their teenager does.

Parents often think of extracurriculars as something that looks good on your college application, which we know is true, but if that's the main reason you want us to do them, we can end up rebelling. We have to want to do them, or else we'll resent you because of the pressure we feel to do something that's more important to *you* than it is to us.

Even worse, parents sometimes want their children to follow in their extracurricular footsteps. Even if that's not what's going on, teens can think that it is. If a father is always talking about what a great soccer player he was and how much he loves soccer, his teenager will hear, "Make me happy—play soccer." If she wants to make you happy, maybe she will—but unless it was what she was going to do anyway, she'll also end up resenting you, or just being very unhappy.

These things can make extracurriculars a very sensitive topic for teens, and parents need to approach it in a delicate frame of mind.

"IT MUST HAVE SLIPPED MY MIND. . . . I QUIT YESTERDAY."

Kyle, a sophomore in high school, is at home watching television in his room on a Wednesday afternoon. His mother, Annette, comes home early from work and is surprised to find that he is not at soccer practice.

"What's going on? No practice?"

"Uhh, no. I just didn't go," Kyle replies, without even looking up from the TV.

"What is that supposed to mean? You just blew it off? You don't care that you made a commitment to the team and now you are breaking it?"

"I'm not really into soccer anymore; I don't feel like playing." Kyle finally looks up and shrugs at his mother as if it's no big deal.

"Kyle, that's ridiculous. If you think you can get away with just quitting, you're highly mistaken. We didn't raise you to be a quitter. You love to play soccer. I don't even understand what you're talking about!"

"You don't know what I love, you know what you want me to love. I hate practice, I hate games, and I hate soccer in general."

Annette is growing more and more infuriated. "You know, Kyle, I've had enough. This is just insane. Tomorrow you are going back to practice and apologizing to your coach. I'm making no excuses for you; you have to learn how to take some responsibility for your actions."

"Thanks, Mom, but I'm not an idiot. I thought about it and realized I don't want to play. I already took responsibility and spoke to the coach a couple of days ago. I'm on top of it, thank you very much."

"Are you kidding, Kyle? Don't you want to be a well-rounded kid? Don't you know it's important that you play a sport? Kyle, you're not a child anymore. You have to think about these things. Playing soccer for a year and a half in high school and then quitting really doesn't look good. How do you explain that you quit an extracurricular and filled the empty spot with nothing but wasting away in front of the television day after day?"

"Look good to who? Seriously, Mom, you have no idea what you are talking about, so please leave me alone. You are being so ridiculous, I can't believe it."

"Your father is going to be so disappointed in you." Annette shakes her head and gives Kyle a final glare before leaving his room.

Saying something like "Your father is going to be so disappointed in you" to a teen is just about the cheapest shot you can take. When you say that you or the other parent is disappointed, your kid will feel upset, angry, and most importantly, ashamed. The shame comes from the fact that he constantly seeks your approval; knowing he has disappointed you and let you down is very upsetting.

At the same time, though, he will get angry at you, because, like Kyle, he has made a choice he believes in and it is extremely frustrating when you, his parents, don't support him. When Annette says, "We didn't raise you to be a quitter," it makes Kyle think his parents, who should be his ultimate support system, aren't behind him.

If teens feel like they don't get support from you, that telling you what's going on only leads to more aggravation, then at some point—whether it's today or a year from now—they will stop telling you things completely. They will either lie to avoid a confrontation or just plain cut you out of their lives. This may sound like a harsh reaction, but the teenage years are a really fragile time, and we teens tend to hold grudges.

Kids can take some advice from parents, but when you flat out say that what they've decided to do or how they're handling a situation is wrong or bad, your kid will really take offense. That can get you into a much more serious situation than just dealing with the original problem, like whether or not to play soccer. Now you are also dealing with the fact that you've hurt your kid and he doesn't feel like you support him. There's a lot of extra stress and tension on the relationship because you said you were disappointed in him.

Even if you really are disappointed, there are better ways to say it than "we're so disappointed," and just walking out. One way to approach the situation is to say, "We wish you had included us in *your* decision, because we would have liked to know that you were having doubts about soccer."

HOW TO MAKE YOUR KID HATE YOU

When Kyle's father, Ray, gets home that night, Annette tells him about soccer. Ray goes in to speak with Kyle.

"So, what's this I hear about quitting soccer?" Ray says, and takes a seat on Kyle's bed.

"That's it. That's the story."

"You just quit without even talking to me or Mom?"

"It's my life, isn't it? You always say I need to take responsibility for my actions, but maybe you don't really want me to. You want to make all my decisions for me. I decided to do something, okay? So why don't you just back off and let me be a responsible adult like you tell me to?"

"Kyle, I never said you can't make your own decisions. I just think we need to rethink this. Calmly. Can we just talk it over?"

"So talk," Kyle grumbles, as he turns back to the computer and starts typing furiously.

"Well, Kyle, it's just that soccer's something you really had going for you. You're a good player and you've been doing it for years. You really showed commitment. It looks good for you. That kind of extracurricular focus really complements your academics."

Kyle whips around from the computer. "Dad, what exactly is all this good *for*? College? Is that what it's all about? Doesn't it matter what I *want* to do? Or is it just about what I *should* do, for college?"

"Of course it matters what you want to do, Kyle, but I don't want you to forget that college is just around the corner. I understand that it's hard to balance soccer and school, but in the long run it's important. You learn a lot from playing a sport. It's been proven, there are studies, kids who play sports do better in school, watch less TV and get into less trouble. . . . Kyle, are you even listening to me?"

"Dad, I hear you. I just don't agree with you. You don't get what I'm saying. I feel like you and Mom never listen to me when I'm talking—you're always asking me if I'm listening, but *you* never listen!

"I don't want to play, okay? I don't want to do high school to get into college, and I'm not a monkey in a test study. I want to enjoy high school. You just don't get it, okay?"

"Kyle, I get it, believe me. I was your age once—"

"Damn it, Dad!" Kyle shouts, interrupting. "It's not the same today. The college pressure, test scores, ex-

tracurriculars—you never had pressure like I do. Please
just let me live my life. It's enough already."

You're right if you're thinking he should have consulted
you. He knew he should have, too, but he didn't for a very
good reason. He knew you would flip out.

We know how upset you would be if you heard from your
spouse that your son had decided to throw away his soccer
career without any warning. But the truth is, if your teenager
was unhappy and stayed with a sport or any other activity because of parental pressure, then he will eventually resent you.

You may believe that it will benefit your child in the long
run if he does extracurriculars because it's good for college,
but insisting will do more damage than it's worth. Every time
you mention the word *college* in a context like that, your teen
thinks, "My parents care more about the college I go to than
the person I really am."

Another big mistake to avoid is taking the "I've been
there, so I know better than you" approach. As soon as you
do that, we think that you are trying to live the life you never
had through us, or you are trying to bring back the good old
days by taking control of our decisions. Your teen will see this
as "I've been there, so do what I did." It's good to relate to
your teen, but not to use it against them.

There are times when it's helpful to remind your teen
that you've been where they are, like when Lindsay gets her
period in chapter 1, but that's very different from using your
experience to force your choices on them. Lindsay's mom
was trying to comfort her. In the situation above, Kyle's dad
is using his experience to bully him.

Of course you would want your son to talk to you about
quitting soccer. Soccer is a commitment, and you deserve to
be involved. Realistically, though, the decision is up to your

teen, so let him know that you respect that, even though you may not agree with him. If you do that, and remember to steer clear of phrases like "it looks good for college," then you are good to go.

Here's what it could look like if Ray takes a different approach.

FACE IT, IT'S MY CHOICE

"What's up, dawg?" Ray playfully asks Kyle, joking around, mocking the teenage slang.

"Hey, Dad." Kyle looks up from his computer and grins at his father's goofiness. "Want to watch *SportsCenter*? I TiVoed it."

"Sure, Kyle, but I want to talk about soccer."

"I should've known." Kyle turns back to the computer.

"Come on, Kyle, don't be like that. It's not a bad thing. Can't we just talk? I want to hear it from you. What's the story?"

"Okay, I'll tell you. Basically, I'm just not into it anymore. I don't like practice, I don't like games, and I don't really like the coach or the other guys on the team. It's just not my thing anymore, I guess. So, anyway, I talked with the coach, explained to him what I just said to you, and he understood. He agreed that it was a good idea to stop if that's how I felt. That's it. That's the story."

"I'm not going to say that I approve of what you've done. I think it was a bad decision to pull out after the season already started. But the truth is, I can't make decisions for you, and if you think it's right, then I'm gonna have to trust your instincts."

"Thanks, Dad. Now why couldn't Mom just get that like you did?"

"I don't think that's fair, Kyle. You've known for weeks that you were going to quit, but Mom and I are just now hearing this for the first time. She needs a little time for it to sink in. You know Mom supports you. She was just shocked. I won't lie. I was surprised too."

"Yeah, I guess. She just bugged out at me before."

"I know, Kyle. You should tell her it hurt you when she did that, but I think she realizes it now. It was just shocking for her. I would have bugged out too."

"Yeah, I guess. . . ."

"Also, Kyle, I think it might be a good idea to look at some other stuff to do in your free time."

"Okay, Dad! I know, okay?" Kyle snaps at his dad a little because he knows Ray is right but doesn't want to hear him say it.

"Okay, Kyle, we can think about it more later."

"Sounds good, Dad. So how 'bout that TiVo later?"

"I'd love to, Kyle."

This is by far the best way to approach the situation. If you come into his room and start a lighthearted conversation, your teen won't feel the need to get defensive. He is more likely to talk with you in a civilized manner, and more importantly to admit he was wrong to get defensive with his mother in the first place.

Another really good thing that Kyle's dad did was to let Kyle know that if he had been in that situation, he would have reacted the same way that Annette did. This makes it clear that Kyle's parents are on the same team, and Kyle can't play one of them off against the other.

Kyle could have interpreted this as the two of them ganging up on him to prove that he is always wrong, but because his dad said it casually, as part of explaining why his mom re-acted that way, it worked well.

Ray let Kyle know that he respected the decision his son had made, even though he didn't agree with it; because of this, Kyle felt like his dad was treating him like an adult. Even if you don't agree with a decision your teen makes, it's always a bad idea to scold him as if he was still a child. All that does is make us stop listening and shut you out, because it really is our life we are talking about, and we take it seriously.

If you treat us like children who need you to decide things, we will give you a hard time (even if we would have made the same decision). When we feel like you hear our opinions, things will end well.

If your teen doesn't react as well to Ray's approach here ("I think it was a bad decision to pull out after the season started"), that's still okay. All the teen can really say is "Well, what's done is done." In this case your response should be, "This is something to keep in mind for the future, because in the real world you can't just walk away from your responsibilities."

Remember, your teen may roll his eyes at this, but that is an extremely effective line to use, because we know you are right.

THE COLLEGE PROCESS IS NOT
THE BOSS OF ME

Robin is a sophomore in high school and her parents have started to think about college. Even though she is not involved in the college process quite yet, her parents want to make sure she is doing things that will benefit her when college applications come along.

Robin has been taking pottery lessons for the past year and a half. Driving Robin home from pottery class one day, her mother, Eve, decides it might be a good time to bring up her concerns.

"So, Robin, I wanted to talk to you about pottery."

"Yeah?"

"Well, I know you have fun doing it, and it's a time when you get to hang out with your friends for a couple of hours after school, but I was thinking that it might be time to take on something a little more serious. You know?"

"No. I don't know. Pottery is serious."

"No, no, I understand, I know you guys enjoy it, but I just think if you took on something like Model UN or debate team or student government it might be more worthwhile."

"But I don't want to do those things. I love pottery. I can't believe you're bringing up college already! I'm in tenth grade! I don't need to think about it yet!" Robin turns to look out the window, frustrated by the constant reminders that she needs to think about college, and that her life is being judged by what will help her get in.

"Robin! I never said a thing about college, honestly. All I said was that in pottery class you and your friends goof around for two hours and never really improve when you could be spending your time doing more productive things."

"What a crock of bull. You're thinking that it will look better when I apply to college if I do debate team rather than pottery class. Well, that's ridiculous, because I enjoy pottery and that's what I want to spend my time doing. Okay?"

"Well, it was just a suggestion. I am just trying to help you, Robin. And in my own defense, I never said

anything to you about college. I know you're in tenth
grade and don't have to think about it for another year
and a half, so please don't act like I'm the one who
brought up college. And don't get mad at me because I
made a simple, helpful suggestion."

"What are you implying?"

"Nothing, Robin. Please, must you be so defensive
all the time?"

Eve and Robin sit in silence the rest of the way home.

Eve blew it. This is what can be called "the ultimate no-no
situation." Saying "It might be time to take on something a little more serious" immediately causes two problems. It belittles
what Robin has chosen and enjoys, which hurts her feelings,
and it raises the specter of college, which Robin knows full
well Eve was thinking of, no matter how much she denies it.

The truth is, it doesn't matter whether you feel college
comes first; what matters is if your teen thinks you care
more about college than about her and her personal interests.
Everyone is already talking about college all the time, so
whether she mentions it to you or not, you can trust that your
teen is aware of what's waiting for her. Right now, she doesn't
need you to point out how weak pottery is compared to being president of her class.

With the pressure of college applications looming on the
horizon, your teen looks to you to be the sane and supportive
one in this situation. She wants you to be the person who hasn't
forgotten about everything but getting into the best schools.

Robin got defensive for a reason. First of all, she's a
teenager, and we take everything personally, which is something you should know by now. But maybe Robin knows that
other things are more "serious" than pottery. Maybe she en-

joys her pottery class precisely because it's a break from the pressures of school and a chance to hang out with her friends. Now she'll never admit it, because of what Eve said. In fact, instead of considering whether she should do something else with her time, this gives Robin the perfect opportunity to turn the situation into one about how her mother doesn't understand her, and she will.

If you think your teenager is a couch potato and want to see her add some "worthwhile" activities to her life, you're going to have to show some discretion in the way you approach the situation. Teens don't think there is anything wrong with you watching out for them, but telling them what's "wrong" with how they spend their time isn't going to get you very far. If they hear about it enough, they'll eventually shut you off completely.

"I WISH PARENTS CAME WITH A REMOTE."

It's a typical weeknight for Jenna, a sophomore in high school. She has been home all afternoon and finished her homework. After she eats dinner, she sits and watches television until ten and then spends some time talking to her friends or playing games on the computer.

Her mother, Cynthia, feels that Jenna should try to find some kind of activity to fill up her time after school. Assuming Jenna will think this is a reasonable idea, she approaches her about it. Jenna is watching a rerun of one of her favorite shows, so Cynthia also assumes this is the perfect opportunity to plop down next to her and strike up a conversation.

"So, Jen, I was just thinking, maybe we should look into some extracurricular activities for you."

"What do you mean?"

TIP

Keep in mind that Robin may be awesome at pottery and this could be her true calling. If this is the case, then Eve shouldn't have interfered in this situation at all, because talent is talent and Robin should pursue what she's good at. So, before you go telling your kids that their activities aren't important and that they should be doing something else, you should be sure you have a really good reason to believe that.

"You know, find some stuff for you to do after school, during the afternoons. I mean, you have so much free time, it's a shame to waste it watching TV."

"I'm not wasting my time. I'm relaxing. I get a lot of homework. I'm only fifteen and I need time to relax. You should realize that."

"Yeah, but there are other things you could be doing with your time, which could also be fun. The world has many things to offer you. You know what I mean?"

"No, I don't. Like what?"

"I don't know. Maybe some kind of club or team? Or volunteering for community service?"

"I'm not into that stuff though. *You're* into that stuff. You do it."

"Well, Jenna, we need to find you *something*. There must be *something* you're interested in."

"Well, obviously I'm interested in TV, America Online and my hair," says Jenna sarcastically.

"I'm just trying to help make your time more productive. It's for your own benefit."

"I'm old enough to plan my own time, thank you
very much. Now if I could just get back to my show??"

Cynthia got almost everything wrong here. When she
says, "You have so much free time. It's a shame to waste it
watching TV," Jenna's offended. What Jenna hears is something like "You have no direction in life, and everything you
do is a waste of time. Why don't you try doing something of
substance? You know, something valuable."

When Jenna says, "I'm not wasting my time. I'm relaxing," the right response is "Oh, I totally agree. You definitely
need time to veg out. I was just talking about something a
couple of times a week, something that you might enjoy. You
know, something you would *want* to do after school." To a
teen, this is *much* better, because it gives validity to the kid's
response, which really *is* valid.

Teens today are faced with more and more responsibility
and pressure. We need a chance to just shut off our brains for
a while, and things like TV and computer games let us do
that. We don't see it as bad or wrong. Even if we don't know
that's why we do it, we know that we need it, and we will not
like it if you try to take it away from us. It's like a survival
instinct.

That's why it's not good to talk about a "productive" activity to replace our vegging time. Instead, you want to say "in
addition," it might be "fun" to do some stuff outside of school
so we're not stuck at home all the time.

Toward the end of the conversation, Jenna has completely blocked out anything that Cynthia has to offer. She
becomes sarcastic to show that as far as she is concerned, the
subject is now closed. Unfortunately for you guys, a teenager
has the ability to end a conversation like this and just write

you off as "ridiculous and unfair," so you must be strategic in your approach.

The low point of this conversation was when Cynthia said, "Well, Jenna, we need to find you *something*. There must be *something* you're interested in." The reason Jenna reacts so harshly to this comment is because she feels Cynthia is accusing her of being inadequate and lazy. Cynthia may mean "I'm puzzled about what might interest you," but to Jenna, it sounds like "You're not interesting."

This would offend any teen to the point that she would shut you out for at least the rest of the conversation, and maybe for a few days. Your teen is now insulted because she thinks you don't get her and she's pissed off because you've made her feel bad about herself. Don't forget that no matter what we say about being treated like adults, or how much we act as if we don't care what you say, *we believe the things you say about us*—even if it's not what you meant to say. Now Jenna feels dumb and boring, because that's the message she got, and she blames you for making her feel that way. Why should she listen to anything else you have to say?

At this point, anything you say will seem like an insult to your teen, and instead of motivating your teen to become active it will cause her to become even more set in her ways.

This is the time to take a breather. The best thing to do is drop it for now. Come back to it, maybe the next day, but definitely not until you have some real suggestions about things to do or at least a plan for how to look for things to do together.

When everyone has cooled down, your teen might even get into finding something else to do—as long as it's something fun or interesting, and not just about doing something "productive," or just about *not* watching TV.

Remember, though, if she even gets a hint of it being about college, she probably will not be into it at all, and she might attempt to chop your head off, which as an activity will not help her get into college. Sorry to tell you, but you're starting out with marks against you. Just the fact that you're bringing it up, even if it's to her benefit, will frustrate her to the extreme.

Your teenager is in a stage where all she wants to do with any free time she has is be a kid, hang out with her friends, watch TV, relax and do other nonproductive activities. If you want to motivate her to do something else, you have to make it about doing something she's interested in.

You also have to let her take the initiative to find something that will be stimulating, and try out different things until she finds the right activity. This means you are going to have to be patient and open-minded. She might try something like volunteering, or debate team, and you will think, "Okay, that's taken care of," but then two weeks later she quits. The first thing she tries might not be the one she sticks with.

Also, she might find something that you never thought of, or that you would never have done. Don't dismiss what she comes up with if it motivates and excites her. She might end up getting an after-school internship at a fashion magazine that introduces her to the world of publishing, when she was really just pursuing her abiding interest in free makeup samples.

The "Best" College for Your Teenager

BOOZE IS NOT AN ACCEPTABLE MAJOR

It is nine o'clock at night, late in September. Jake, a senior, needs to hand in a list of the colleges he is interested in, in order of preference, to the college office tomorrow morning. Frustrated with his choices, Eric, his father, decides it's time to talk to Jake about the way he's weighing his options. Eric thinks that Jake is choosing colleges based on how much of a party school they are.

"Jake, don't you think you could be a little more selective with these schools?"

"Selective? What are you implying?"

"Well, Buffoon State College isn't going to give you the same quality of education that the University of Rochester will, so why isn't Rochester on your list? Your college advisor said that you have a pretty good chance of getting into Rochester. Why settle for something like Buffoon State as your first choice? It has nothing to offer you except booze."

"Dad, I don't like Rochester. Have you not been listening in the meetings? I keep telling you, I'm not considering Rochester. Why are you pushing so hard for this?"

"Because it's a damn good school. It has more to offer you intellectually. Why don't you challenge yourself for once? You'll be happy anywhere you go, so why go to a school that can't offer you the same things academically?"

"This isn't about challenging myself, Dad! This is about being happy! I know you want the best for me but why don't you take a hint and just *butt out! It's not your choice*, it's mine!"

"Yes, it is my choice, as long as I'm the one paying your tuition."

Every parent has his own idea of what school would be "good" for his child, and it's completely understandable that you don't want to spend money on tuition when you think your kid is just going to drink and slack off. But the truth is that we can drink and slack off anywhere. By forcing a student to go to a specific college, all you do is give him a reason to rebel and go even crazier at the school of your choice than he would have at the school of his choice.

Teenagers know that you have their best interests in mind and they don't hate all your input. It's how you give it that matters. Offering your advice is one thing, and something we recommend, since you are older and more experienced, but making threats and issuing commands is not something we advise; it can only lead to a series of battles that you will ultimately lose.

For example, when Eric says, "Yes, it is my choice, as long as I'm the one paying your tuition," he may mean "Hey, consider what I have to say, don't ignore me," but Jake hears, "What you want doesn't matter, the decision is in my hands, so don't even bother filling out this list, I'm going to control your life." And when Eric says, "Why don't you challenge yourself for once?" Jake hears, "Everything you've done up until now has been worthless."

Here's a much better approach to helping your teenager.

> "Jake, I know the college advisor thinks you should apply to Buffoon State, but do you really see yourself in that environment?"
>
> "Yeah. Obviously. Why else would I apply there?"
>
> "All I'm saying is that you haven't really looked into anything but the social life on campus. I know that campus life is one of the most important aspects of college, but maybe you should look on their Web site tonight, go through their course catalog and make sure there's stuff that appeals to you.

"I know it's far in advance to be thinking about what you would major in, but you should just make sure they cater to your interests."

"Yeah, but I have seven spots to fill on this list. I may as well put it down and deal with that stuff later, Dad."

"But there's a possibility that you may find out Buffoon doesn't offer the classes you want, and ten other schools do, and you will have missed your chance to apply. I mean, honestly, any college can offer you booze, so you may as well make sure that the academics interest you as well."

"Yeah, okay, maybe."

"It's just something to think about. I'm looking out for you. I know you have a lot of work tonight, so if you want my help, I'm in the next room. I could save you some time on those boring Web sites and get you the info you need."

"Thanks. I'll see."

The best thing that Jake's dad did in this conversation was to offer his help. Since he is the one that is so fixated on Jake not applying to Buffoon State, he takes on a little of the responsibility and offers to make it easier on Jake. Good move. There are no guarantees that this approach will work and change Jake's plans, but if you offer your help, it at least eliminates that objection.

You don't want to be overbearing and controlling, but your input is helpful in situations like these. Your teen may not be thinking eight steps ahead; he may be thinking only two steps ahead, so it's helpful for you to put everything into perspective and help paint a clearer picture.

When Eric says, "There's a possibility that Buffoon doesn't offer the classes you want, and ten other schools do, and you will have missed your chance to apply," Jake hears, "I'm just keeping track of the details and trying to help you out, but I won't make any decisions for you." Great! Jake may not have thought of it that way, so Eric's suggestion really comes as a helpful eye-opener instead of a controlling comment.

If you follow this scenario closely, you have done all you can do without damaging your relationship. The major part is just throwing the idea out there, and now you just have to step back and let the teen figure it out for himself.

MAYBE I SHOULD HAVE GOTTEN HIM A MUG?

This past weekend was Ed's twenty-fifth college reunion. At the school store, he picked up a couple of things, including a Princeton sweatshirt for his seventeen-year-old son, Jack. On Sunday, when he got back, Jack was out at a movie, so he left the sweatshirt on Jack's bed.

When Jack gets home he finds the Princeton sweatshirt sitting on his bed.

"What is this?" Jack asks his father.

"Oh, I got that at the reunion. We need some good old Princeton spirit in this family—"

"Excuse me. Why did you get this?" Jack says, interrupting.

"I got it because I thought you might like wearing your dad's college sweatshirt. If you don't, that's fine. I just thought you'd be proud of your old man and his roots."

"Oh, *right*. I know you have all these high hopes about me and Princeton, Dad, but honestly, thanks but no thanks. I really don't want this sweatshirt."

"Jack, where do you come off talking to me like this? What's your problem?"

"Dad, it's enough that I have to deal with other kids telling me I have a Princeton legacy, and you and Mom always hinting at my Princeton future. I really don't need a sweatshirt that advertises all this crap, too. I'm tired of always talking about college and Princeton and all the rest of it. It's enough already. Jeez."

"What's wrong with going to Princeton and being proud that your parents went there? It isn't a crime, you know."

"You just don't get it. I don't want it, okay? I really don't ever want to talk about this again. Is that so hard to understand?"

"Yes, it is. I see nothing wrong with a Princeton education and I see nothing wrong with wearing a sweatshirt that says the college name. It doesn't have to mean anything if you don't want it to. You shouldn't let your friends make you feel bad about something like this. They are probably jealous."

It makes sense that Ed wants Jack to follow in his footsteps; after all, he's set a pretty solid example by attending Princeton. But Ed steps over some serious teenage boundaries here when he says things like "I thought you'd be proud of your old man" and "You shouldn't let your friends make you feel bad about something."

When a parent says something that involves the word *proud*, the teen is thinking, "So you're going to try to manipulate me? I'm not stupid enough to fall for that crap." In this situation, you can count on a teenager to do the exact opposite of whatever the parent wants.

Second, when a parent suggests that a teen is being bullied into something by friends, or that they're doing something just because of peer pressure, you are entering a realm where you will encounter a large amount of teen resistance. When Ed says, "You shouldn't let your friends make you feel bad about something like this," what Jack hears is a challenge. To Jack it feels like his dad is daring him to stand up to his friends by wearing a sweatshirt that Jack never wanted in the first place. Jack thinks that Ed is insinuating that he's weak, spineless, *and* he picks bad friends. We shouldn't have to tell you that, once again, this is the perfect way to get your kid to do the opposite of what you want.

The first thing parents need to realize is that constantly reminding your kids of where you went to college is always a

TIPS

- Be aware that your teen does want to impress you and live up to your standards, but try not to take advantage of that, because it will only backfire.
- As much as you may want your teen to go to Elite University, you need to convey to him that whatever his decision is you will be one hundred percent behind him. It's okay to tell him that you are personally drawn to a school, as long as you let him know you will respect his personal preference as well.
- Try not to bring his friends into your arguments; if you are talking about college with him, then he should be old enough to handle his friends.

turnoff. If another person says, "Wow, your dad went to Princeton?" it can give your kid a sense of pride, but when it comes from the parents themselves, it feels like you are trying to control them. Worse, it can be intimidating. It makes a kid feel like his parents have a standard he must live up to, and that he'll disappoint his parents if he doesn't.

It's okay to set challenges for your teens academically—"I bet you can't ace Mr. Johnson's math test"—as long as you know your teen has the *potential* to ace the test, but it's a very bad idea to set standards that are impossible or unfair.

Every teen seeks his parents' approval in some way, shape, or form. The trick is not to set standards that are too high. Suppose Jack ended up going to Princeton because he wanted to make his dad happy and win his approval. If things didn't work out for Jack at Princeton, socially or academically, then he would blame it on his father and the resentment would be almost impossible to reverse.

Here's another way that conversation could have gone:

> When Jack gets home he finds the sweatshirt sitting on his bed. "What is this?" Jack asks.
>
> "Oh, I got that at the reunion. I hope it's the right size."
>
> "Why did you get this?" Jack says, interrupting him.
>
> "What? You don't like it?"
>
> "Oh, *right*. I know you have all these high hopes about me and Princeton, Dad, but honestly, thanks but no thanks. I really don't want this sweatshirt."
>
> "Jack, it's a sweatshirt. That's it. I thought you would like it."
>
> "Dad, it's enough that I have to deal with other kids telling me I have a Princeton legacy, and have you and

Mom always hinting at my future at Princeton; I really don't need a sweatshirt that advertises all this crap. I'm tired of always talking about college and Princeton and all the rest of it. It's enough already. Jeez."

"Calm down, Jack."

"No, Dad. You just don't get it. I don't want it, okay? I really don't ever want to talk about this again. Is that so hard to understand?"

"Okay, Jack, sorry. I didn't realize it was such a sensitive issue. Maybe your sister would like the sweatshirt."

Ed handled this situation perfectly. There was nothing a teenager could interpret as offensive in Ed's reaction. Ed stayed calm when Jack acted irrationally, and let him get out all his anger. He wasn't defensive. Ed knew that the insults weren't really about him—the whole scene was about what Jack was going through: "I didn't realize it was such a sensitive issue."

If Ed had said, "Jack, sit down and listen to me, I want to explain to you right now how much I don't care whether or not you go to Princeton," Jack wouldn't have heard a word he was saying. Even if he did, Jack wouldn't have believed it. He would have thought it was a trick to get him to go to Princeton. Either way, he would have bugged out even more. It was a good move on Ed's part to let Jack vent and then walk away from the situation.

If Ed doesn't say anything, how will Jack know that Ed doesn't care about him going to Princeton? Ah, the beauty of a follow-up conversation. All Ed has to do is bring up the topic again, once Jack has calmed down. He can say something like this:

"Jack, you seemed upset earlier about the sweat-shirt. I bought it for you because I thought you'd like it, not because I want you to follow in my footsteps and go to Princeton. I am one hundred percent behind your decisions and I would never intentionally pressure you into going to Princeton or anywhere else you didn't want to go. I'm sorry if I made it seem like that to you, but I want you to know that I didn't mean to upset or hurt you."

Ed could even have e-mailed something like this to Jack. Either way, though, this should do it.

Chapter 3

"But Everyone Else Is Going!":

Curfew and Other Issues That Go Bump in the Night

Even though it looks like they do, kids do not really want to set their own boundaries. Teenagers don't want to say it, but we really need guidance from our parents because we know we can't set safe boundaries on our own. We know that our parents' experiences will help protect us from making mistakes; it's just not the kind of thing we will ever admit.

Curfew

"BUT HER CURFEW'S LATER!"

It's a noisy Friday night in the Fox household. Lara's been invited to sleep at her best friend Rachel's house with three other friends, but Rachel's curfew is an hour later than hers. When it's just Rachel and Lara going out, they go home early to make Lara's curfew, but tonight everyone wants to stay out later. Although Lara already

knows the answer is no, she decides to ask her parents
to change her curfew anyway.

Jan and Steven, Lara's parents, already know the
question she's going to ask and say "No" before she even
finishes asking the question.

Upset, and also embarrassed by how predictable she
is, Lara bursts into tears and starts attacking her parents.

"Just because you didn't go out when you were
younger doesn't mean I should have to pay for it! You
guys are so unreasonable! All my friends have cooler
parents and later curfews!"

Your kids *do* want to be restricted. They understand that
it is appropriate for them to have a curfew. They know it's for
their safety. But they're still going to push you until they hear
what they want to hear.

Keep in mind that *understanding* is key when dealing with
curfews. Even if teens can get as far as hearing *what* their parents say, they often overlook *why*. It's easy for teens to nod
their heads when you speak, but what you really want is for
them to understand your reasoning.

Parenting is often like the advertising business—you need
to sell your idea to your teenager and make him understand
your position. A clue that you've gotten your teen to actually
listen is when he asks, "Why?" This shows that he is absorbing the rules.

A word of warning: the most common response to
"Why" is "That's the way it is. This curfew is appropriate for
somebody your age." You should know that in a teenager's
mind, this is not a valid reason, and it will not get a good response. Two other common responses that trigger terrible
feedback are "When you live under my roof, you abide by my

rules" and "I was your age once, and I know what teenagers do as it gets later."

Instead of these lame responses, which could end up making things worse, here are three practical approaches to the curfew issue that could make your life and your teenager's life more pleasant:

1. You know your teen's friends have different curfews, some earlier and some later than your teen's. Your teen constantly compares himself to the friend with the latest curfew. You take it upon yourself to call your teen's closest friends' parents. Together, you set a standard curfew. It doesn't matter what this curfew is; your teenager no longer has the opportunity to make you the bad guy.

   A bonus is that if your teen sleeps out, you know exactly what time he'll be in for the night. You're running a risk here, though. If your teen finds out you have been plotting with other parents behind his back, he will not be happy. (See below for how to handle that situation.)

2. If your son or daughter's friends have later curfews you don't approve of, and your teen is suffering because of it, cut a deal: it will make him feel like he's negotiating and in some sense "winning," even if you have already decided how this will all turn out. If he wants a later curfew all the time, offer him once a weekend or once a month. This will probably leave your teen satisfied, not just with you but with himself. Keep in mind this satisfaction will be temporary, because he still hasn't gotten everything he wants, and teens never stop until they get exactly what they want.

3. If your main concern with your teen being out late is drunk driving, find statistics and articles that make you

cringe, because they will probably do the same to your child. Cut the articles out. Leave them on the kitchen table for a few days. Eventually your teen will pass the article, and even if she chooses not to read it, a glance at the headline may do the trick. This technique will hopefully help your teen to understand that it isn't always her you don't trust; it's the other people on the road you think are dangerous. She may be responsible enough not to drive drunk or get in a car with a drunk driver, but that doesn't mean the driver in the other car is sober.

"I KNOW YOU TALKED TO HER PARENTS! I HATE YOU!"

Heather is fifteen and always complains that her curfew is hours earlier than her friends'. Her mom, Laura, decides it's time to find out if Heather is telling the truth, because she wants to know if the curfew she has set is truly unreasonable.

Laura calls Heather's friend's mom, Karen, and together they decide that the curfews these days have been getting out of hand. Laura keeps Heather's at the same time and Karen makes her daughter's curfew earlier.

The following day, Andrea, Karen's daughter, comes to school and freaks out on Heather. Embarrassed that she isn't even aware of what's going on, Heather tries to defend herself by saying her mother would never do that. Really, though, she has no doubt that her mother did it, and that night, Heather goes home and confronts her.

"How could you call up Andrea's mom? You barely know her! Now Andrea's curfew has been changed and it's all because of you. It's one thing to make my life miserable, but you don't need to go around making my friends' lives as bad as mine. Now Andrea hates me!!" Heather screams at the top of her lungs.

Laura tries to reply reasonably.

"It was just two parents talking and she agreed that the curfew was inappropriate to begin with, so she wanted to change it, Heather. I didn't tell her to do anything. I was just checking to see if it was me who was unreasonable about your curfew and it turns out I wasn't."

"Yes, you are! Just because one parent came along and agreed with your ridiculous theory that fifteen-year-olds shouldn't be out past eleven doesn't mean that you are right. You have not only ruined my nights out but now you have ruined my friendship with Andrea. Way to go, Mom."

Yikes. If you aren't friends with the other parent, then don't call. It's one thing if your teen is going over to her friend's house and you want to call and say, "Thanks for having my child over. What time will they be coming home tonight?" It's another thing to just call randomly to talk about curfew.

We fully support calling a parent you are friends with, because friends talk about things in their lives, and your teen will understand this. But when you go around talking to parents you aren't friends with, not only will your teen feel betrayed, she will be in trouble with her friends. Your intention may not be to "screw up her life," but that's how she will interpret it. She will see this as "My mom doesn't want me to have a social life. It's like she wants all the kids in school to hate me. How could she do this to me?"

"HOW COULD YOU TALK TO JAN
ABOUT THAT?"

When Nancy decides it's time to find out if Rachel is telling the truth about her curfew, she calls her good friend Jan, who is also the mother of one of Rachel's friends. The two mothers talk about their daughters' curfews and other kids' curfews and what is and isn't reasonable.

In the end, they decide that curfews in their daughters' crowd have been getting outrageously late, and maybe even dangerous. Nancy keeps Rachel's curfew early, and Jan decides to change her daughter's curfew from twelve thirty to eleven.

The following day, Emma, Jan's daughter, comes to school and freaks out at Rachel. Embarrassed that she isn't even aware of what happened, Rachel allies herself with Emma, apologizing for her mom and labeling her as a "total psycho." That night, Rachel goes home and confronts her mom.

"How could you call up Jan? Now Emma's curfew is an hour and a half earlier and it's all because of you. It's one thing to make my life miserable, but you don't need to go around making my friends' lives like mine. Now Emma hates me!" Rachel screams at the top of her lungs.

"Rachel, that's not fair. I was only talking to my close friend. I was asking her for advice. Don't you ever ask your friends for advice? I didn't call Jan so she would change Emma's curfew, I called her to set up a lunch date and we ended up talking about curfews. She decided on her own to change Emma's curfew when she found out what I thought. We're two grown women talking. You don't actually think that I could persuade her to change her mind if she didn't want to, do you? Besides, you know we're good friends and good friends talk about important issues, and I know that curfew is an important issue to you."

"Well, you just put my friendship on the line, so I wouldn't really know much about good friendships, would I?" Rachel spits out.

"Look, you know that I would never intentionally jeopardize your relationship with Emma, and you know that she will only be angry for a day or two. It's just not fair for you to accuse me of this when all I've done is talk with a good friend about why you have an earlier curfew. If you want, I'll talk to Jan and she can tell Emma that you have nothing to do with it, and she shouldn't be mad at you."

"You've done enough already, thank you very much."

If you were talking to your own friend, who happens to be a parent of your teen's friend, you have done nothing wrong. In this conversation when Nancy says, "I was asking her for advice. Don't you ever ask your friends for advice?" she challenges Rachel to make a parallel between her friends and her mom's; this is awesome. It forces Rachel to be realistic about the situation. Instead of giving a long rationalization, Nancy cuts to the chase and says, "Wouldn't you talk to your friends?"

Between this and hearing what the conversation was really about, your teen will realize that you are not to blame (which, keep in mind, could potentially make her even angrier, since it's always easier for teens to blame their parents and not take responsibility for the circumstances).

She may not say to you, "Oh, okay, Mom. You're right. I

shouldn't be mad at you, because you weren't out of line at all. It was all my fault. I apologize." Who wants to give you the satisfaction? But if your teen walks out of the room when you explain this to her, she probably realizes that your actions were completely justified. She is no longer mad at you, but she doesn't want to admit she was wrong.

"BUT EVERYONE'S GOING!"

This time Lara is staying over at Hilary's and has asked her parents to change her curfew so she can stay out later with the rest of her friends. When her parents say "No," Lara starts attacking them.

"Just because you didn't go out when you were younger doesn't mean I should pay for it! You know, you guys are so unreasonable. All my friends have cooler parents and later curfews! It's so unfair!"

"Oh, please, Lara, that hasn't worked before. It's not going to work now."

"Please just hear me out. Tonight is supposed to be a fun night because it's midsemester break, and Hilary's camp friends are in from Canada and it would mean a lot to me to get to stay out tonight. Please, you guys, it's not fair."

"We set your curfew for a specific reason. We think that this is an appropriate time for someone your age to be home at night. Any later and we would be breaking our own rules. You can't ask us to do that."

"Fine, I understand that you aren't going to let me stay out later tonight because you don't believe it's safe, but in the future, if I show that I am trustworthy and never break curfew and behave exactly how you want, can we please discuss making a later curfew? Not that I haven't already shown you that I'm responsible. It's not like I hang around on the street. I don't understand why a half an hour makes such a big difference!"

"Look, you're right. We're not going to let you stay out later tonight. But you're also right that you have shown you are trustworthy and responsible, so we have a proposition for you. If you continue on this positive track for the next month and all of spring break, then we will give you one night a month when you can stay out later than your normal curfew. But that's only if you give us enough warning, like by dinnertime, and if you tell us where you're gonna be."

"Really? What if my reason is I'm having fun and I want to stay? I won't know in advance."

"Well, why don't we try it this way first? If you aren't abusing this privilege, and you're responsible enough, then we can discuss it. We're giving you an inch, so don't you try to take a mile. We'll revisit it *after* spring break."

"Fine, whatever."

This went well. Compromising is a good strategy because your teen can't scream and yell at you without feeling foolish because you've just given her a privilege that she didn't have a minute ago. It may seem as though teenagers will continue to push for the "right" response, ignoring any compromises you propose, but you just have to let them keep asking until they wear themselves out.

You're probably thinking, "If they don't appreciate the compromises I'm willing to make, why do it at all?" We *do* appreciate them. We are grateful and excited, but we are still teenagers! After all, we wanted to get a later curfew right now, not to compromise about the future. So you're just going to have to sit back and keep saying "No" until we absorb it and finally hear "No" instead of "Keep pushing, maybe they'll cave in."

One thing you can do to shut us up after the fifth time we ask is say, "If you ask the same question again, then we'll take back the offer and you're not going out tonight at all." This threat will definitely stop us. We'll keep going until we finally push you to your limits, and this lets us know that we've found them.

Repercussions for Coming Home Late

"THAT'S SO UNFAIR!"

Jane is sixteen years old and has an eleven o'clock curfew. It's ten thirty on a Friday night and she's with a couple of friends at an older friend's house. The older friend doesn't have a curfew, and her other friends have curfews later than hers. There's nothing going on that her parents wouldn't approve of, but she's having a really good time and isn't ready to leave. Jane knows she should watch the time so she isn't late for curfew, but the other kids have just turned on a movie that she's never seen, and she gets caught up in it.

Just before eleven, Jane looks at her watch and gets her stuff together and leaves. She knows her parents will be waiting when she gets home, and when she opens the front door fifteen minutes after eleven, there they are; her mom is pacing back and forth while her dad sits by the phone.

"I'm sorry! I lost track of time. I know what you're going to say. I'm sorry." Jane tries to make the situation better before her parents even say a word.

"Jane, this is completely unacceptable. You have a curfew for a reason and if you're not going to respect it then you can forget about going out at night from now on," her father says, with that disappointed look in his eyes.

"I'm sorry. We were watching a movie and I lost track of time and—"

"Sorry is not good enough. You're late and Dad and I have been worrying all night. Dad's right, you're not going out for the next two months—"

"But, Mom!"

"This isn't an open discussion, Jane."

"Mom! That's so ridiculous. I'm only *fifteen minutes* late, so you couldn't possibly have been worrying 'all night.' And that's so unfair! I'm fifteen minutes late and I can't go out for *two months*? You two are so out of line!"

"No, Jane, I think you are the one who's out of line. Now why don't you go get ready for bed? We can talk more in the morning."

"Don't bother! I'm never talking to you again in my entire life!"

Being late for curfew might be a serious problem, but there's no reason Jane and her parents had to get in this large a fight. The very first, preemptive way to avoid this entire situation is to talk about repercussions before Jane even steps out the door.

When you sit down with your teen at the beginning of the school year or the beginning of the summer or whenever you set a new curfew, you should also outline the consequences that go along with coming home late. This way, when your teen is late for curfew she knows what to expect. She'll still get angry, but she'll know that it's her own fault and be aware deep down that she's to blame.

In this case, Jane wouldn't have gotten so angry, and there wouldn't have been such a big fight, because she would already have known that by being fifteen minutes late she would lose her late-night privileges until the end of the year.

If you take this approach, the one time you might still experience bickering with your teen is when you are setting out the consequences, because teens won't want to even hear about the possibility of losing privileges. In the end, though, it's better to fight once at the beginning, when things are more open to discussion. If you wait until your teen comes home late, she'll feel outraged and will not listen to a word you say.

If your teen comes home late and is shocked and angry to find out that the punishment is more severe than he ever imagined, it is still possible to avoid a major fight. The key is to stay as calm as possible, because then your teen can't yell and get upset without looking like the irrational one. If you stay calm while you explain how you are feeling and what the punishment will be and why, your teen will probably still be mad, but he won't blow up in your face. He knows that he messed up and that you are being completely rational, so even though he will probably act pissed off and walk away, he won't yell and scream.

Also, try not to double-team your teen. Jane's parents both told her how disappointed they were and how her apology didn't cut it; this wasn't necessary. Although we are big fans of having both parents present so the teen can't play one parent off the other, it's a bad idea for both of the parents to state how unhappy they are. One is enough.

And don't repeat yourself! All you will do is piss your teen off and she will stop listening to what you are saying.

The trick to a successful argument is to make it short and sweet. If you are redundant, you are inviting your teen to shut you out.

A MORE POSITIVE APPROACH (EVEN IF THE RULES WEREN'T LAID OUT BEFOREHAND)

Jane walks in the door fifteen minutes late.

"I'm sorry! I lost track of time. I know what you're going to say. I'm sorry."

"To tell you the truth, that's unacceptable. Your curfew is in place for a reason."

"I know, but I just made one mistake. This is the first time."

"That's true, but that doesn't mean we're going to just ignore it."

"Yeah, I know. So what are you going to do?"

"Well, your mother and I will have to talk it over a little more, but it looks like you'll be grounded for two months."

"That's way too long! Are you out of your mind?"

"No, Jane, not really. Curfew is a serious issue—you know that. We're not just going to let you get away with this. You have to understand that we're not flexible about curfew, because it's a safety issue for us. We've been sitting here worried and waiting for you. This is our way of making you understand that."

"I understand, though. I know I messed up."

"We know you understand, but there are consequences, and for this situation the consequence is two weeks."

"All right, fine. I get it."

Jane may not act all happy and dandy, but this was a good conversation because her parents stayed calm, and only one parent spoke. This kept Jane from completely losing it.

Staying calm is the first secret to avoiding a major fight. The second is to recognize and acknowledge that your teen knows she messed up. Giving her credit for admitting to mistakes and not trying to make excuses will benefit you, because your teen wants to be seen as a mature person. Once you do that, she no longer feels forced to challenge anything and everything you say.

Jane's father acknowledged that she was taking responsibility for her own actions when he said, "We know you understand, but there are consequences, and for this situation the consequence is two weeks." When you acknowledge that your teen understands she messed up, she no longer feels like you are the enemy. Instead of seeing your punishments as mean and unfair and just the flexing of your parental muscles, it seems to her like you are all talking it over like rational adults.

We know we will end up being punished and we know you are being reasonable, because we *did* break a rule. But when you recognize our maturity and stay calm, rather than automatically start yelling and screaming, we feel we are being treated like equals. We may even feel like we had an influence on the punishment, which will make it more likely that we will not freak out on you.

THE BEST APPROACH (WHEN THE RULES WERE LAID OUT BEFOREHAND)

Jane walks in the door fifteen minutes late.

"I'm sorry. I know I messed up. I just lost track of time. I really didn't mean to be late."

"That's right. You had me and your mother worrying. You lost track of time and now you know the consequences."

Movies

Some critics hold movies and other entertainment responsible for the violence of today's teenagers. Because of this, many parents have attempted to prevent their children from going to see certain R-rated movies, or any movie with sex or violence, afraid that they will have a bad influence. For those of you who think your teen isn't seeing these movies just because you have forbidden them, or because kids under seventeen aren't allowed into R-rated movies, you are fooling yourselves. If your teen is smart, he will nod his head and pretend he understands and respects your feelings about this just to avoid a fight, and then he will turn around the next day and go see it—with a fake ID, if necessary. He knows he can't change your point of view, so he isn't going to waste his time or energy fighting about it.

On the other hand, some teens will argue about it, even if they don't really care that much. These are the ones who feel that being told they can't see a movie represents a greater issue—of autonomy—and they want to take a stand. Their thinking goes, roughly, "This isn't about movie X. This is about my parents thinking they can control my life and that I'm not old enough to make my own decisions."

Then there are teens who don't even want to see a specific movie until you've said, "You can't see this." Then he will go because he wants to be the rebellious, "living on the edge" type of teenager. Your teen wants to prove to you, and the rest of the world, that he is old enough to run his own life and that you need to stop trying to do it for him.

If you don't condone your teen going to see a certain movie, then obviously you shouldn't give him money to pay for it. This sends the message loud and clear that you don't think it's appropriate but you've accepted that your teen is old enough to make a decision like this on his own. Also, you can say to your teen, "I know you don't really care, but I just want you to know why I think this movie isn't worth your time." Your teen will hear you out, and might even learn a thing or two.

Just don't be naïve and think that your teen is automatically obeying your rules just because he is smart enough to nod his head and say, "Yes, Daddy."

"Yeah, I know, okay? Grounded for two weeks and no TV. We talked about this, I know."

"All right, honey. Now why don't you try to get some sleep?"

"Ugh. Good night."

Okay, so it might not be this perfect, but it won't be much worse, because she *did* have fair warning and already knew her punishment. There really wasn't much for her to argue about. The worst that could happen in this case is if she acted mad at you because she was frustrated with herself, but that would be gone by the morning.

Another thing about making all the rules and repercussions clear in advance: your teen will be more careful about being on time and making curfew when she knows what's at risk. It becomes something she will respect for her own benefit, even if not for yours.

Looks like an Excuse to You . . . but Not to Your Teen

Jane's situation is pretty common. Because she was only fifteen minutes late, not an hour or more, she acknowledged that she was late but blamed it on losing track of time. Your teen might blame it on something else innocuous, like traffic, or another friend holding him up, or miscalculating how long it would take to get home.

The first thing you need to realize is that teens don't look at these statements as *excuses*, but more as *explanations* for why they are late. We aren't trying to say that these things mean we shouldn't be punished, we just want you to know that we are not completely careless or disrespectful of your rules.

When you hear these explanations that sound to you like excuses, it's probably hard to stay calm, but *try*. The best thing you can do is tell your teen to get to bed. If you discuss it now, when you are both heated, it won't be a discussion; it will be more of a screaming match.

In the morning, start the conversation by saying, "I know you didn't mean to be late for curfew." Say that you know it may have been an honest mistake, you too made the same mistakes as a kid, and you know how much it sucks to be punished, but you feel you just can't let it go without taking some kind of action. This way your teen will at least feel heard and understood.

If normally she is respectful of curfew, don't forget to tell her that you appreciate it and you just want her to be more careful in the future. If you don't, she will probably think, "What insensitive jerks. I screw up *once* and that's all they care about." She will definitely be more accepting of your punishment if she knows that you know she is trying.

What Exactly Is a Reasonable Punishment for Breaking Curfew?

Of course, your teen won't admit to you that the punishment you set for breaking curfew is a good one, but there are some punishments that will get more respect than others.

Only you can say what seems reasonable for your kids, but our advice is to not overreact. Being grounded for several months will make us so frustrated and so pissed that we won't even try to respect these consequences. We may deal for a week or two, but once we realize we're not even a tenth of the way through the grounding, we're going to be angry, antsy, and ready to sneak out of the house. You need to make a consequence that will be respected and will teach the lesson, without making your teen hate you.

This is another reason to talk over repercussions with your teens before they go out. Although they won't *like* any punishment, you may learn which ones they accept as reasonable and which ones they wouldn't respect for more than a week. If a teenager doesn't think it's reasonable, it won't do its job, so talking it over with your teen can really help to get an effective outcome. All you have to do is say, "What punishment would you give if I did this? And be honest. . . ."

Another thing to avoid if you want us to cooperate is having just one punishment for being late, whether it's ten minutes or two hours. It's important to acknowledge that there are different gradations of breaking the rules. You might also want to make contingency plans, for when missing curfew is due to circumstances beyond our control.

For example, you might want to make a five- or ten-minute flex period. This way, your teen isn't penalized for being five minutes late due to traffic or anything like that. The flex period obviously shouldn't be so long that it's like having a later curfew, but it would be there for the rare occasions when your teen is running late. This is an especially good idea if your teen is always on time for curfew and respects your other rules. When you give us a few minutes' leeway, it takes off a lot of pressure and we know you trust us.

If you are having trouble communicating with your teens about where they are going at night, ask them to check in at certain times, or ask them to check in when they switch locations. This way you know where they are at all times and what they are up to. Phone calls leave less room for miscommunication, but make sure not to smother them with rules. The more rules you create, the easier it is for your teen to begin to break them or forget half of them.

Calling in might sound like something your teen would never agree to, but don't make it an option. If it makes you feel comfortable, then we should call. We know it isn't an unreasonable request. It's also a good way to prevent breaking curfew because your kids are kept on track over the course of the night.

Some Key Things to Remember

Try to outline repercussions beforehand so that you and your teen are on the same page. Even if you haven't before, and you've had many fights about curfew, it's never too late to sit down and make all the rules and repercussions clear to your teen.

Set times for your teen to check in with you along the way.

Consider making varying punishments for different degrees of breaking the rules (e.g., a different punishment for being fifteen minutes late than for being an hour or more late).

When your teen *does* come home after curfew, try to stay calm. When you stay calm, teens know you are only being rational and doing your job as a parent, whether they acknowledge it openly or not.

If you can't stay calm at one-thirty in the morning when your teen was supposed to be home and in bed two hours ago, you can express your disappointment or anger or frustration, but try to keep it to a minimum. Come back to the situation in the morning when you've both had a chance to cool down, and your teen has hopefully had a chance to think over what happened.

In any situation when you have to reprimand your teen, don't forget to tell him you recognize the positive things he is doing (there must be *some* positive things). Knowing that you understand he is trying will make him feel better and can help him accept the punishment.

"Do as I Say, Not as I Do": Smoking and Drinking

Smoking

The first thing we have to tell you about smoking is this: if you smoke, you should quit. If you don't want your teenager to smoke, you have to stop smoking. One of our favorite things to do is notice that adults are hypocrites, and no teenager will ever take anything you say about smoking seriously as long as you smoke.

The next thing you need to consider is how much your opinion matters to your teen. You might be surprised to hear it, but it is often a parent's opinion that matters most. That's a main reason teens do not trust or confide in their parents. A teenager has a defensive mind; we're always thinking about ways to protect ourselves by keeping information from our parents. Although you may find this hurtful, it's actually the biggest compliment a teen can give a parent. We care about our parents' opinion so much that we hide things, fearing you will not approve.

Now that you know, burn this sentence into your brain: *If your teenager is hiding something from you, it's probably because he knows you wouldn't approve.*

If your child is hiding something like smoking and you manage to stumble upon it, ask him up front, "Why did you do it?" Your teen probably won't admit he knew it was wrong; instead he'll say something like, "I didn't think about it." Without even realizing it, he has set himself up. Quick, recite the sentence: "If you didn't think about it, then why did you bother to hide it? You must know it's wrong if you feel the need to hide it."

If you always bear this in mind when the time comes to confront your teenager, it will be easier for you to stop accepting his excuses. Your teen knows you want to believe him and can sometimes try to take advantage of that. This statement is a reminder of the facts, not the warped story your teen may feed you.

When you find cigarettes or other incriminating things in your teen's personal space, it helps to remember that to him the situation is a personal privacy issue (see chapter 1). Teens won't see the issue the way you would. Teenagers will interpret this as their parents plotting against them, so you'll have to address that before you can put the focus on the real problem, their health.

"DO YOU SMELL A LIAR?"

It's seven in the evening and David is late for a business dinner. Adam, David's fifteen-year-old son, borrowed David's tie for a sweet-sixteen party and apparently didn't have the time to return it. Now aggravated, David goes to look for the tie in his son's chaotic room. As he searches frantically for the tie it occurs to him that Adam may have put the tie in the hamper.

Reluctant to dig through all that dirty laundry, David cleverly flips the whole thing over, allowing its contents to fall to the ground. Lying at the top of the laundry pile is a half-empty pack of cigarettes and a lighter.

Outraged at the idea of Adam smoking and hiding it from him, David decides to call Adam's cell phone and interrogate him about the cigarettes.

"Adam, I was looking for my tie in your room—"

"You went in my room?"

"You forgot to return my tie, Adam, and I had to—"

"It's in the bathroom. Can we talk later? I'm going into a movie."

"Adam, I found your cigarettes."

Dumbfounded, Adam hangs up. David calls back. No answer. He calls again—the phone has been turned off.

Worried that Adam will do something dramatic or drastic, David calls his business associate and says he has a family emergency and will have to cancel their dinner.

Three and a half hours pass. The movie should have been over for a while, yet Adam's phone is still off.

The first thing that went wrong was when David tried to talk about it over the phone. It's practically impossible to maintain parental control over the phone. Look what happened—Adam hung up.

By using the phone, David gave Adam the power to walk away from the problem, instead of trying to resolve it. Just like everyone else, teenagers find it easiest to avoid a situation rather than to confront it. If David really felt the need to confront the situation immediately, he could have asked Adam to come home and told him what was up when he got there.

Another reason Adam hung up the phone is probably because he didn't know what to say. Either they were his cigarettes and he wasn't sure whether to admit it, or they were not his cigarettes and he couldn't very well squeal on someone when his friends were standing right there listening.

The truth is, though, that teenagers sometimes *want* to be caught and confronted. This lets them know that their parents are paying attention. If a teenager happens to be a smoker, he doesn't want his parents to be okay with it. Accepting it is one thing, but approving of it is another.

Often, when teenagers act out by smoking, doing drugs, drinking, and so on, they are asking for their parents to set boundaries. They don't want their parents to overlook these behaviors. Although it may make them seem like "cool" parents to other kids, to the most important person, their own teen, it seems like they no longer care.

It is important to address these sorts of issues head-on, but you still need to be careful how you go about it. When David said, "I found *your* cigarettes," Adam interpreted this as an accusation. If David eliminated the word *your* and said, "I found cigarettes" or "I found cigarettes in your laundry bin," Adam would think there was a chance to explain, and might not hang up the phone.

WHAT TO DO IF YOUR TEEN IS HONEST ABOUT SMOKING AND EXPRESSES INTEREST IN QUITTING

When Adam returns home, his father is anxiously waiting for him. Adam walks into his room, where he finds his dad sitting on his bed, and starts fidgeting with his keys, avoiding eye contact with his father, waiting for him to say something. Finally, Adam starts talking. "You shouldn't go into my room without my permission, but . . . I'm sorry."

"Are you implying that those cigarettes are yours? Or are you saying you're sorry because you hung up on me?"

"Uhh . . . both, I guess," mutters Adam as he begins to walk away.

"So that's it? You think 'sorry' gets you off this hook?"

"Well, what exactly do you want me to say?"

TIP

Like Adam, other teens have headed down this path long before their parents noticed. How can you tell if your child has started smoking?

Does he often go out for walks in the evenings during the week?

Does he come home smelling like cigarettes? (If the answer is yes, it still doesn't mean he smokes; it could be his friends, or where he was hanging out.)

How often have his friends been over to the house lately? Has he been hanging out with different kids?

"You can start by telling me when you picked up that nasty habit."

"I don't know, just a few months ago. But I don't smoke during the week, just weekends. I tried to quit."

"Yeah, it's hard. I've been there. Once you start, it's hard to go back. Do your friends smoke?"

"Uhh, some do."

"God, Adam, do you even want to quit? Or is this some social competition?"

"I just told you, Dad, I *tried*, but it's hard! You just said so yourself!"

"Well, you're going to have to try harder."

"I know I should quit, okay?"

It's easy for teens to put on a face for their parents and tell them what they want to hear, but your teen may be saying "I'll quit" only to shut you up. You must not stop talking about the issue.

When Teens Say Sorry

Let's assume Adam says he wants to quit and has already apologized for having hidden his smoking. Just
because he has said all the right things and appears
to have all the right intentions, it still doesn't mean
he can walk away from the situation.

If you let your kids off the hook just because they
say "sorry" you are allowing them to think that these
simple words can erase their previous actions. Not to
say they don't mean it, but teens have a really easy
time saying "sorry" because they also know it's an
answer for anything and it's what you want them to
say. The first baby step may be apologizing, but teens
must understand that that isn't the end of it.

It is not exactly shocking news to teens when parents say
"smoking is bad for you," and making them feel guilty is only
a temporary solution. Don't think lecturing your teenager
about smoking is all you have to do. This just lets the teen
walk away thinking, "I'm off the hook. All I had to do was
pretend to listen to him for five minutes!"

When Adam said, "I know I should quit," the key word
was *should*. This isn't the same as saying he *will* quit. Just like
he knows it's bad to smoke and he still does, he knows he
should quit, yet he still hasn't. In this situation, David had the
chance to really make Adam face the facts and ask: "Do you
really *want* to quit?"

First, realize that because habits like smoking or drinking are not casual in the same way watching too much TV is, it will make matters worse in the long run if they are treated casually. Allowing your teen to walk away from this situation after making what could be an empty promise may seem like the easiest solution, but your teen will interpret that something like this: "My parents don't care enough to help me. Why should *I* make the effort if *they* don't? All I need to do is find a new hiding spot for my cigarettes and pretend I quit. If they didn't notice the first time, why would they notice now?"

So be blunt. Confront the situation straight out and state plainly what you expect him to do, even if the immediate reaction will probably not be pleasant. You're going to have to be hard on him, not only to prove that you care about him but also to force him to live up to the promises he makes.

Try not to react to your teenager's feelings about the subject until you've gotten your point across. Most importantly, don't let your teenager hijack the conversation and manipulate you with distractions like "But, it's so hard, Dad," or "I was really hurt that you went through my stuff without asking."

All teens know that the best tactic when it comes to their parents is gaining sympathy. Although you may feel sympathetic, it's best to hold the mushy stuff until they understand what is actually expected of them. Teens need their parents to be blunt about something like this. It's the only way the message gets across loud and clear.

Keep in mind that no matter what you choose to do, your teenager is not going to thank you . . . at least not now. But, *please*, don't say, "You'll thank me later." To teenage ears, this sounds like "I'm going to be condescending right now because I am right and you're just a kid who isn't mature enough to understand."

Some Methods Your Teen Will Respond To

1. Offer to pay for part or all of a nicotine patch or nicotine gum program. But it can't just end there—you need to stay involved. Keep reinforcing the reasons why your teen is quitting, otherwise the temptation to fall back into old habits can become too strong for him to resist.

2. Take him to a cessation program for teens. In this setting, your teen has a chance to identify with other people his own age going through the same things. Plus, there may be some things that your teen is not comfortable talking about with you; he may be more comfortable telling other people who don't know him as well as you do, and who he feels would be less likely to judge him.

3. Not always, but many times there is more to the smoking than meets the eye. So even if you get him to stop smoking, you might not be dealing with the root of the problem. You might want to look into finding a psychiatrist, psychologist, social worker or other professional your teen can talk with confidentially about other issues. There are a lot of things surrounding a teen's social life that he probably will not feel comfortable telling you, whether it concerns his friends or his own habits. Also, a professional will be more objective than any parent could be, and an

outside perspective is often enlightening to a teenager. (This will probably work best if he agrees to go rather than if you force him to go kicking and screaming.)

WHAT TO DO IF HE'S HONEST ABOUT IT BUT SHOWS NO DESIRE TO QUIT

When Adam returns home, his father is waiting in his room. As Adam begins to fidget with his keys, David becomes irritable.

Finally, Adam says, "What are you doing?"

"What am *I* doing? What have *you* been doing for the past five hours?"

"I told you I was going to the movies," Adam snaps.

"You think it's going to go away without even talking about it?"

"Well, what exactly do you want me to say?"

"You can start by telling me when you picked up the nasty habit of smoking."

Adam doesn't respond, except by glaring at his father.

"Adam, I was a smoker at one point, you can tell me."

"Fine, I smoke sometimes . . . but only to relieve stress . . . stress that you and Mom create."

"God, Adam, you brush it off like it's nothing. Do you even want to quit?"

"Not really. I can control it. Anyway, I'm not addicted."

"Everyone starts out that way, until one day you
wake up with a headache because you haven't had a
cigarette."

"Dad, I'm not asking you to understand, but it's my
body. I think I've been pretty respectful, not smoking
under your roof, but just like I show you respect, you
need to show me some by accepting who I am. So lay
off it already."

So you're impressed. He's finally being honest about who
he is. But do you like who he has become? Probably not.

You have a chance to really change things, but you need
to be ready for a fight, because a teen who is thinking this way
is certainly ready for one. Keep in mind that he does not
want to hear what you have to say. He will just shut you out,
like Adam does when he dismisses his father's warning,
"Everyone starts out that way . . ."

In a couple of years, your child will be in college, and by
that time, you hope, you will have raised him to make wise
and informed decisions. Now, during the teenage years, is
when you are trying to teach him how to do that. Often,
teenagers will pretend they are not listening, but don't stop
just because we act like it's going in one ear and out the
other; we are actually absorbing a lot of what you are saying,
we just don't tell you so.

Your teenager is still living under your roof, so even if he
doesn't use the information you provide him with, it won't
hurt him to show you some respect by listening. Don't allow
him to shut you out or manipulate the situation. Say something like "It can't hurt to listen to what I have to say on
the subject, and you may even take something away from it.
I'm willing to listen to whatever you have to say, so you need

to listen to me." Don't count on this as a tactic to stop him from smoking. This is just your chance to try to make an impression.

Unfortunately, the final decision isn't yours to make. If a teenager doesn't understand why he should quit and make that decision on his own, then in two years, when he's away at college, he will just revert to the same habits, and probably on a greater scale. If teens don't understand and appreciate the rules you've set (about curfew, homework, drinking, etc.), and just think of them as things you make them do, they will see college as a time to catch up on all the things they have been "missing out on"; they will overcompensate, which can only hurt them in the long run.

You probably consider your rules fairly lenient and appropriate. You can't imagine your teen going wild at college because you've been an accepting parent all along. When your teen studies really hard for a test and still gets a bad grade, you probably say something like "It's okay, as long as you tried your hardest." The same attitude can apply to things like smoking.

When you talk to your teenager about smoking, here's an approach you may want to take: "I'm never going to approve of your smoking. You know just as well as I do how unhealthy it is. I know that you have already made up your mind and you think my opinion doesn't matter, and you are not going to want to hear my nagging for the next twenty years. But as a parent, I can't accept you smoking without making one last attempt.

"I want you to have all the information about all the consequences that accompany smoking, so for the next couple of weeks, you will attend a smoking program. It won't necessarily be one that asks you to quit, but it will give you the information you need to make an informed decision. If you attend this program and still decide to smoke, I will leave you alone. I still won't accept it, pay for cigarettes, allow it in my home, or anything of that sort, but I'll stop trying to make decisions for you."

You are the parent, so it makes it harder for teens to admit you're right. A smoking program may provide your teen with a more objective and informative perspective, one he might respond to better.

A TACTIC TO MAKE HIM COME CLEAN IF HE SMOKES AND HIDES IT FROM YOU

When Adam returns home, his father is waiting in his room. "Sorry," Adam says. "I shouldn't have hung up. Those aren't my cigarettes, but I couldn't say that because my friends would think I was a snitch and they were standing right there."

"Why should I believe you?"

"Have I ever broken your trust?" Adam asks, challenging his father to call him a liar.

"No, but don't you think it's a little suspicious that you were hiding them? Why do you even have them to begin with? If you were with your friend tonight why didn't you give them back to him?"

"I wasn't sure I was going to see him tonight and you really caught me off guard when you called."

"I'm sorry. I didn't mean to do that to you, but I got nervous when I found them."

"It's OK. I understand. You made a mistake just like I did. I should have been honest with you."

"Yeah, okay, son. Good night." David gives Adam a hug and distinctly smells cigarette smoke in his hair and on his jacket. A little suspicious, David pulls away from Adam.

"If you didn't bring your friend his cigarettes, why do you smell like smoke?"

"He bought another pack."

"Adam, I can't help being suspicious about your actions when the people you spend your time with smoke. I promise I won't be mad if you tell me that you smoke sometimes; I just need to know the truth. You know how I feel about lying. If I were to find out that you've been smoking, I would be really angry because you weren't honest with me."

"Okay, I've tried it. I don't really smoke. It's not like I'm addicted."

It's easiest for a teen to admit something when he doesn't feel like there is a consequence or lecture to follow. In this circumstance, David handled the situation perfectly. He made the act of smoking casual while making honesty the focus. He doesn't take the issue of smoking lightly, but by putting the emphasis on lying, he offers Adam a safety net.

Teens will often respond to an approach like this one because they see it as an opportunity to gain "bonus points" for being honest. They know they'll have to deal with the smoking issue later on, but the scenario seems less intimidating to them. Teens have a defensive mind and this system allows parents to get a foot in the door and cause teens to be more open.

Although this method is ideal, there are plenty of kids who will still not admit to smoking. They might be in denial themselves and think they're not addicted, just a weekend or social smoker, or they might still be scared of the consequences, no matter how light you make it sound.

If you think your teenager is smoking and he still won't admit it, you may want to keep an eye out for changes in behavior for the next month or so. A month may seem like a long time, but there's a good chance you have scared or guilt-tripped your teen into not smoking for a while; once a month or so passes, he may fall back into old habits.

If no evidence has surfaced and your teen still hasn't admitted anything, it's probably in everybody's best interest to leave the topic alone. If you continue to push, your teen will interpret it as a serious invasion of privacy, which will push him further away from you. Teenagers become especially defensive when they feel like they are being interrogated. We can only be asked the same question a certain number of times before we start hearing, "I don't believe a word you're saying so I'll keep asking until you say what I expect."

Drinking

Even if the way we act makes it impossible for you to notice, we teens look up to you. What you do, we want to do, and if it looks like having a few drinks is your way of taking the edge off at the end of the day, then many teens are going to think, "A drink or two may help relax me, too."

Yes, you are legally allowed to drink and we aren't, and yes, it is totally different for a fifty-year-old to have a glass of vodka than it is for a thirteen- or sixteen-year-old, but we don't look at it like that.

To be honest, we teens don't look at very many things realistically. There is often little logic involved in our thought process. It's as simple as this: we see you drink, and maybe even lose control, so we see nothing wrong with doing it ourselves.

The first thing that you can do if you want to teach your teen how to be a responsible drinker is stay away from saying things like "I could really use a drink," or drinking enough to slur your words or stumble. You don't want to get messy in front of your children, because it sends the message that drinking an extreme amount of liquor is okay when you are an adult.

All teens want to grow up quickly, so if you drink a lot and they want to act older, then the obvious thing for them to do is have a lot of liquor. So try not to reminisce about the funny thing that happened that time you got drunk. Even if it's just casual conversation at the dinner table, your teens will remember it and it will make them think that drinking too much is a fun and social thing to do rather than an irresponsible one.

Beyond setting a good example for your teen yourself, there is only one other thing you can try to do before they actually start drinking (which they *will* start doing at some point). You can train your teen to associate liquor with bad experiences and lame people. For instance, you have a friend who was kicked out of the prom for drinking, and it ruined their last high school experience. Also, casually mention the effects of alcohol. Whether you can see it happening or not, your teen will be absorbing any details and stories he hears from you, and hopefully they will have an influence later on, when he is given the opportunity to drink.

Here are three different scenarios where it is easy to slip in a life lesson or two.

"ONLY DRUNKS ACT LIKE THAT!"

Andrew and his father, Steve, are sitting around
watching the Yankees / Red Sox World Series game on

TV. All of a sudden a fight breaks out in the stadium and the cameras are turned toward two men with painted faces punching each other in the stomach while security tries to break them up. An announcer says that security will be escorting them out of the stadium as soon as it is possible to do so.

"What schmucks," says Steve, a little ticked off. "They are screwing up our game."

"Yeah. They look like morons dressed like that."

"Only someone drunk would dress like that and make a complete fool of themselves. Maybe if they cut down on the booze they wouldn't miss the best game of the series."

"Yeah. Sucks for them."

All it takes is a sentence or two. As long as the message is "alcohol made them act like that," then you are set. If teens learn from the beginning that alcohol makes people lose control and make bad decisions, then they are more likely to become responsible drinkers. Stories are especially effective; teens are less likely to forget them and many times they pass the stories on to friends. You might not convince your teen that underage drinking is "wrong," but if you leave him thinking, "I don't want to be kicked out of the basketball game" or "I don't want to be suspended and banned from the prom," that could be motivation enough.

"DON'T YOU THINK SHE'S DISGUSTING?"

Amanda is sitting at the table with her father, Tim, and her mother, Monica. They are having a casual discussion about their neighbors, the Rydells, and how rude their children are.

"Their kids aren't respectful when they are in our house," says Tim.

"They aren't respectful when they are in anyone's house."

"Amanda, why don't you like them?"

"I don't know. They just aren't nice."

"It seems that everyone has noticed their rude behavior. Cathy, the youngest daughter, has even come home drunk many times," adds Tim with disgust.

"Figures. Bad kids with bad habits," adds Monica.

"Yeah. The Greenes have nice kids, though. I think we should invite them over for the Super Bowl. You think so, Amanda?" asks Tim.

"Yeah, that would be really fun."

This sends the message that drinking isn't approved of, but it also refers directly to teenage drinking, as opposed to the first scenario, where the teen might not identify with the people on TV. The only way you can have this conversation and make it successful, though, so that it doesn't sound preachy or as if it's directed at the teen, is if you do it casually, and don't turn it into a lecture. This way you can get your message across by playing off of your teen's dislike for the other teenagers.

When you are looking for a scenario to discuss with your teen, you should try to find one that she can identify with, or one that will really freak her out, like a drunk-driving accident that happened in your area recently. But please remember that you don't need to add a moral to the story at the end of the conversation, like "So make sure to be careful when you cross the street." Your teen isn't dumb, and she has already drawn that conclusion without you verbalizing it.

When you say it out loud, it looks like you purposely told the story to prove some point and scare the living daylights out of your teenager. Which you did, but the more obvious you make it, the less effective it will be. After you have this conversation, try to move on to something else, like Tim did by bringing up the Super Bowl.

"REMEMBER THAT TIME . . . ?"

Martin and Mindy are reminiscing with their two teen daughters, Glinda and Patty, about their college days and how much fun they had. It's obvious that wine plays a role in their family because Martin is an avid collector, but Mindy makes sure to only have one glass of wine with dinner.

"Yeah, we had some good times, but not at first, because we didn't know our limits then," Mindy says, with a sigh.

"What do you mean, Mom?"

"Well, when we first got to college, we were really irresponsible and stupid. We had never been around alcohol before, so it was exciting to us. I thought I was invincible when I first got there, but I learned the hard way that I wasn't. The first few times I went to a party, I would just drink like a fish. I didn't regulate myself, and that was a really big mistake. I almost ended up in the hospital. I was dumb and I didn't take care of myself. I pushed my drinking limit, and I ended up spending hours puking afterward. I thought I could be like people I saw on TV or in movies and drink, drink, drink, without losing control, but I couldn't. I quickly learned that two drinks was my limit. After that, I started losing control."

"That must have sucked."

"Yeah, it did, and it sucked for everyone around me, also. People started to not want to hang out with me, because they knew I drank too much and they didn't want to be responsible if something bad happened. Fortunately, I learned, just like we all do, and now I know how to handle my drinks, as you can see."

"Yeah."

This is an extremely effective approach, because it makes your teen identify with you, but it is also quite challenging. You can't make up a story to teach your teen a lesson, because she will eventually find out if it wasn't true; teens find out almost everything. You must also be careful with the story you choose because you don't want to dig yourself too deep a hole. The first time your teen gets trashed, he might turn around and say, "Well, you drank and you were stupid about it, so cut me some slack here."

That's why you have to choose a story about a short-lived or one-time mistake that illustrates how you learned your lesson. This way your teen knows that even if you do cut her slack for a first mistake, you're not going to let it slide again.

The reason you want your teen to identify with you when it comes to drinking is so that she will feel like you are on the same team when she makes a stupid mistake. She'll think you can help, since you've been there, and that makes it much more likely she'll be honest with you.

Also remember that if you choose to tell a drinking story, you don't want to tell it while you are on your third glass of wine at dinner. All the story will do then is call attention to your drinking habits instead of teaching your teen to drink responsibly.

So, how do you choose the right story to tell? Well, it should be about you, or one of your close friends—as long as you have all the facts straight. It shouldn't be too wild, like "Let me tell you about the time I got drunk and killed the family pet," because even if it really happened, that isn't the kind of thing that can be written off as a drunken mistake, and you wouldn't want to give your kids the idea that it is.

The story also needs to be a pretty common experience, something that your teen may have already witnessed a friend go through, like driving drunk or throwing up on somebody's porch. They need to relate in order to grasp the larger purpose of the story: drink responsibly.

By the way, the reason we keep saying "drink responsibly" and we aren't saying "don't drink" is because that wouldn't be realistic. It's realistic for you to request that your teenager not drink, but it's unrealistic to think that she never will. If you teach responsible drinking, it will be a lesson that goes a much longer way, because at some point your teen will probably have a drink. This will help her do it more safely, because she will be prepared. Telling her not to drink will only leave her defenseless when she finally does drink, and she will. Whether in college or at age thirteen, it *will* happen, and you need to be prepared for it so you can help your teen reach the right conclusions about the effects of alcohol.

"HOW DARE YOU COME HOME LIKE THIS!"

One Saturday night, sixteen-year-old Sandra walks into the house at around one o'clock in the morning. Normally, she knocks twice on her parents' door in order to tell them that she's home, but tonight she doesn't. A little aggravated, her dad, Danny, gives her a few minutes to remember.

Five minutes go by and there is still no knock. Instead, Danny hears a few bangs and what sounds like either a clumsy daughter or a robber. Danny decides he'd better check on Sandra.

To his surprise, he finds her just sitting at her computer doing what she normally does—nothing. Annoyed that he got out of bed just to find nothing the matter, he sharply asks her, "Why didn't you knock?"

"What do you mean? I did knock," she says, defensively.

"No, Sandra, you didn't," says Danny, although he is a little unsure of himself, since it is one o'clock in the morning and he was sleeping.

"Yes, I did, Dad," Sandra says, slurring her words.

"Are you drunk?"

"No." Sandra looks down.

"Yes, you are. Tell me what you did tonight."

"I just went to the movies, Dad," Sandra says, slowly and carefully.

"Then where did you get the booze from?"

"I didn't get any alcohol. Are you calling me a liar? I can't believe you don't trust me. Get out of my room!"

"How dare you lie to me! I asked you a question, now answer it truthfully. I was your age once. I'm not stupid. You are slurring your words like a drunken fool. *Now* be honest, because I *will* find out, and when I do there will be serious consequences—because you lied, and not because you drank!" shouts Danny at the top of his lungs, waking up the entire house.

"I had a few drinks," whispers Sandra under her breath.

"*How could you come home to this house drunk and disappoint us like this!* Drinking is a disgusting habit that we do not approve of. I hope you realize that there will be serious repercussions. Now get to bed!" Danny shrieks.

If you want to get through to your teen about drinking, you don't want to have this conversation. Although Danny touches on a few important things, like "don't lie to me because lying will only get you into more trouble," he goes about it in the wrong way; he shouts, and he buries his point with insults and accusations like "drunken fool" and "how dare you lie to me."

What Sandra is hearing is "I am so ashamed of you; you're so irresponsible; and even though I know you're drunk, I'm still going to ask you a zillion questions." Teens will focus on the insults and accusations and try to turn everything around on the parent, instead of focusing on themselves and how they shouldn't have come home drunk to begin with. All that Sandra will be thinking is "Next time I'll just sleep at a friend's house so I don't have to put up with this crap."

Also, Danny shouldn't have jumped down Sandra's throat once she came clean about drinking. No, she shouldn't have been *praised* for being honest, but she is not going to be honest ever again if it results in *"How could you come home to this house drunk and disappoint us like this,"* especially after Danny just said that he wanted her to be honest. Sandra will be thinking, "That's the last time I'm honest with them. If it's going to get me into more trouble, then why should I tell the truth?"

This conversation should have ended after Sandra admitted that she'd had a few drinks. Danny should have replied, "Okay, let's talk about this tomorrow, when we are all thinking clearly and we can make a rational decision about the consequences." We strongly recommend you wait to have the conversation, because if she is drunk, chances are she won't remember half of what you say, and your chances of having a positive effect on her future decision making are lower.

This first incident is really a blessing to you, especially if your teen gets sick, because it's your chance to step in and say, "I've been there, I've done that, just like you have, and now let's come up with a way for you to be a little more responsible." Try not to ruin this opportunity by yelling at her and making her feel bad about herself, because this chance only comes around once.

A BETTER WAY: "I'M NOT STUPID. I KNOW YOU DRINK."

After Sandra admits she had a few drinks, her dad tells her to go to bed; they'll discuss it the next day. The following morning Danny sits down with Sandra to talk about responsible drinking.

"Sandra, we need to talk about what happened last night."

"Okay, talk."

"Listen, I'm not stupid. We both know that you are going to drink whether I give you my approval or not. You know how I feel about it, but I was sixteen once and I know that it doesn't really matter what I say. You're going to be around alcohol, and you'll probably drink no matter what I say."

"So?"

"You probably know most of my drinking tips but I'm going to tell you anyway. It makes me feel better to tell you, since I've already been through the process of learning my limits. I have gotten sick because I've ig-

Some Key Tips About Drinking

You know they will drink, so teach them responsible drinking.

1. Don't drink if you haven't eaten, because you will get really sick.
2. Learn your limits. Don't keep drinking because you don't feel the effect; it can take a while to hit you, so drink slowly. This way you can feel when the alcohol is beginning to affect your judgment.
3. Don't drink and drive, and don't get in a car with someone who has had *anything* to drink. They may not realize it yet, but the alcohol has affected their judgment.
4. Don't ever put a drink down in a bar or at a party where you can't see it, because a date-rape drug or any other type of drug can be slipped into it.
5. Don't take a drink from a stranger or someone you don't trust, for the same reason.
6. Don't drink from a punch bowl, for the same reason.

Illustrate these tips with stories—they don't need to be your own, just true—so teens can understand more clearly why you think it is important for them to know these things before drinking.

nored those limits, and I feel the need to pass down my knowledge, because I know you wouldn't want to lose control of yourself."

"Okay, go for it, Dad."

The Secret to Getting Through to Your Teen

If you really want to be effective when you talk to your teen, the *most important thing* for you to say before launching

A Word About Drugs

No matter how protective you are, your kids will be exposed to drugs. The best thing you can do to prepare them for these encounters is to talk to them the same way you did about alcohol. Remember, you don't want to be overbearing. Spitting out hundreds of statistics and facts all at one time on why drugs are bad won't help your case.

If you think your teen is doing drugs regularly, there are programs and counselors that you should look into. This is beyond negotiating with your teen; if you see that your teen isn't being receptive, you must look into the programs even more quickly than you would with drinking or smoking, because teens are not equipped to deal with addiction on their own.

into your preachy speech is "I know you understand these drinking precautions already, but I'm your parent and it's my job to reiterate them."

Why is this such a good way to open up the conversation? Because teens think they know everything and you know nothing. If you start off by saying, "I know you probably know this stuff," then they are more likely to listen to what you are saying. If you don't, chances are that when you make your first point, your teen will respond, "I already know that!" and then shut your next five points out completely.

A Final note on Drinking

Some teens may be drinking regularly, or you might have repeatedly talked to your teen about drinking and he still comes home drunk. More serious help may be required, such as a teen drinking program, a school counselor or a psychologist. There are many resources to turn to, and if you think your teen has a serious drinking problem, you should look for professional help.

Chapter 4

"I Wish I Were an Only Child":

Brothers, Sisters & Friends

Maybe you decided to have another kid so that your first kid would have a built-in friend. You probably had visions of brothers and sisters playing together and helping each other with homework, or an older brother taking care of a little sister or brother who looked up to him as a hero.

That may have been the plan, but what you really did was supply your kids with a built-in pest. Here are two things you should know. Teenagers will always insist on choosing their *own* friends, and siblings fight. The chance that you will approve of everyone your kid hangs out with decreases after twelve and gets worse every year. And when you have more than one child living at home, you're bound to experience some form of sibling rivalry—everything from fighting over the remote control to screaming battles about each other's personal lives.

Now that you've created this situation, you have to figure out what to do about it. It's hard enough for parents to know when to get involved in their children's business, and it's even trickier when the business is between siblings. Nothing we tell you is going to stop brothers and sisters from fighting, but we can tell you what's really going on with your teenagers when they fight with their siblings, and that will give you a better chance of figuring out when and when not to get involved.

Siblings

Separate but Equal

"YOU LOVE HER MORE!"

Fourteen-year-old Ellie and her seventeen-year-old sister, Beth, have just finished eating dinner with their parents, Nancy and Stanley. The whole family helps to clean up; Stanley clears the table and wipes it clean, Nancy washes the dishes, and Ellie and Beth are responsible for packing up leftovers and drying and putting away the clean dishes. The family rule is that nobody gets dessert until dinner is completely cleaned up.

After packaging what's left of the salad and putting away the milk and juice, Beth, unnoticed by her parents, reaches into the freezer, grabs an ice pop, goes back into the dining room and sits down to start eating it. Seeing that neither of her parents has said anything to Beth, Ellie proceeds to do the same thing and grabs an ice pop of her own.

"Hey, hey, hey! There's still chicken and potatoes to be put away, missy. Put the ice cream down."

"Are you kidding? Do you see Beth eating ice cream right in front of your face? She hasn't done squat—"

"Just do it, Ellie! Don't make this such a production, please. Who cares who did what?"

"But, Dad, just because I'm the one left standing doesn't mean I should have to do Beth's half."

"Ellie, it'll take you two minutes. Stop complaining."

"Argghhhh! You're sooo unfair!" Ellie slams down the ice pop. "I can't stand it! This is ridiculous, absolutely ridiculous," she mutters as she goes back to finish cleaning up.

Okay, this conversation might seem completely bizarre to you, because you don't see the problem. Sure, Ellie gets upset, which is bad, but there's no reason for it—isn't this just the usual irrational teenager behavior? Well, maybe, but there's something more to it. Although the conversation appears to be mundane and quite benign, the fact is that Ellie feels like she is not being treated equally; she feels like Beth can get away with murder, while she can't even leave a dish unpolished.

When Stanley says, "Just do it, Ellie! Don't make this such a production, please," Ellie hears, "You're a baby. I'm not sensitive to your feelings and I don't really care if I'm being unfair." It might seem irrational that Ellie interprets it this way, but she can't help it; sibling rivalry is a powerful and touchy issue. Favoritism is a common perception among teens with siblings, and it needs to be dealt with sensitively and carefully.

Unfortunately, sibling rivalry can be triggered by little things that you wouldn't expect to be a problem, so it's difficult to prevent it. There are some things you can do to help your cause, though, and in a case like Ellie's, the first thing to do is have a follow-up conversation to see if your teen really thinks you favor one sibling over the other. It's important to have the right follow-up conversation, so don't make these mistakes.

FOLLOW-UP: WHAT NOT TO SAY

"Ellie, what was that exhibition at dinner tonight?" asks Stanley.

"What do you think, Dad?"

"I honestly don't know. I don't see what we did wrong at all."

"Well, I can't be the parent and point this out all the time. If you don't see that you favor Beth, then you have a serious problem."

"Now, that's ridiculous, Ellie. You know I don't favor Beth or you. How could you think that? You're just making up reasons for me to get mad at your sister."

"Oh, wow. Gag me. You are completely lying. There you go again, taking Beth's side and making her look like the innocent victim," snaps Ellie.

"Okay, Ellie. You are totally out of line. How dare you accuse me of being a liar? When you can act your age and talk more civilly about this, then maybe we can resolve this misunderstanding."

Yes, teens can be dramatic, but Ellie really couldn't help it, and Stanley made the situation worse by calling the scene in the kitchen an "exhibition." Ellie now hears Stanley accusing her of being a drama queen and blowing everything out of proportion. This not only makes her feel stupid, it automatically makes it harder to have any kind of positive follow-up conversation. It was smart of Stanley to wait for Ellie to cool off after the interaction in the kitchen, but now Ellie will shut down, and she's no longer calm enough to have an honest, rational discussion about her sister and how she feels about favoritism.

When Stanley says, "I honestly don't know. I don't see

what we did wrong at all," he should follow up with "Please tell me so I can understand the way you are feeling." Without this last part, Ellie is thinking, "My dad's clueless and he doesn't even care enough to ask why I'm so upset. Instead he's spending his time telling me he's done nothing wrong."

Stanley's absolute worst move was saying, "You're just making up excuses for me to get mad at your sister." *Wow.* That's a strong statement, and quite a damaging one. There's no turning back after that. Ellie will definitely not be speaking to her dad for a couple days. Of all the places Stanley could have gone in this conversation, defending Beth is the number-one worst choice. When Stanley did this, Ellie hears, "Beth's feelings are my priority and what I'm *really* concerned about is that the issues we are having will hurt her. You, on the other hand, I'm not worried about."

To top this disastrous conversation off, Stanley then insults Ellie and tells her to grow up. Not like the damage hadn't already been done, but there's nothing like an insult to make sure that Ellie's self-esteem plummets to the ground. It's true, Ellie was disrespectful to call Stanley a liar, but she was being defensive because she had clearly been hurt by his previous comments.

Now that Ellie has told Stanley she feels like Beth isn't doing her chores around the house, things can get even worse. If Stanley goes into Beth's room and says, "Ellie was right tonight. You don't do your chores," or "I now realize that you have neglected your responsibilities around the house recently," Beth might nod her head and say, "You're right, Daddy, I'm sorry," but when she's done talking to Stanley, she is going to march herself right into Ellie's room and say, "Thanks, you little brat. It's your fault that Dad's on my case about chores now."

You don't want to set your teen up so that she's in a more vulnerable position than she was already. It was hard enough for Ellie to admit how she felt about your relationship with her and her sister; you don't want to add to that the weight of having Beth blame her for what you do. Teens rarely accept responsibility for their own actions; if your daughter has a chance to blame a sibling for her problems, she is going to seize the opportunity with open arms. The following approach is your best bet for avoiding that.

FOLLOW-UP: HOW TO FIX IT

"Ellie, what was going on at dinner tonight?" asks Stanley.

"What do you think, Dad?"

"I don't know. You seemed really upset and I want to know what I can do to help."

"You can stop favoring Beth."

"Now, Ellie; you know I don't favor Beth or you. I love you both equally."

"Feed your lying sob story to someone else," snaps Ellie.

"That's not fair."

"Not fair? What's not fair is how Beth can get away with murder and still be your perfect angel, but for me, I need to do my chores *and* her chores before I can just have an ice pop."

"Ellie, I'm sorry. I didn't realize at that moment what Beth was doing, but you shouldn't have been getting dessert either. But I admit it, she deserved to get yelled at just as much as you did."

"Yeah, she did."

"Okay, well, I will try to pay more attention from

now on. Are there any other circumstances that you can think of when I have been unfair? Because I really don't mean to be and I'd like to make things better."

"No."

Stanley was right to admit his mistake. He also made a good move when he said, "You know I don't favor Beth or you. I love you both." Even though Ellie's response was really obnoxious, she does like to hear those words. Parents really need to say "I love you" to their kids *all* the time—everything from saying "Love you" when you hang up the phone or leave the house for the day to coming into your teens' rooms as they're falling asleep to tell them one last time that day how much you love them. You should try to do this individually with each of your kids, and make sure that nobody is getting more attention than anybody else.

If it isn't already a habit, you should make it one, because even the two or three words mean a lot to your kids. Also, it can't hurt to actually make the point that you love all your children equally—just make sure that you aren't accusing your teen of thinking you don't love her. She'll just say, "I never said you didn't love me!" and she'll probably be embarrassed that you can "read her mind" so well. Just say something like "I know you know this, but I love you and each of your siblings just the same and that's more than anything else in the world." Even if your teen knows you don't *really* love one of your kids more than another, she can't help feeling inferior at points, and you have to make sure not to belittle this feeling . . . *or* accuse them of it. Your teen wants your reassurance without being singled out as the kid who *actually* thinks that she isn't loved.

You might be thinking this is ridiculous because you tell

your kids you love them each and every day and they know it, but it's important to remember that you need to individualize it. Make sure that you treat each kid with the same love, and don't just group all your kids together into a ball.

So, why did Ellie say, "Tell your lying sob story to someone who cares"? Well, she's thinking, "You say you love us equally, but your actions are telling me something totally different." Listen to your kids when they say things like "You never treat Beth like that" or "Why do you always blame me?" Even though you may completely disagree with your teen, this is how she feels; this is the message she is getting from you and you need to deal with that.

If you respond by saying something like "Oh, that's ridiculous, you know I treat you both exactly the same," your teen hears, "You're so immature and you don't know what you're talking about. Just stop complaining." Your teen feels like you don't respect the way she is feeling, which makes her even more frustrated and upset. You have to take the things she says to you seriously. That doesn't mean it has to become a big issue, but you have to recognize that how she's feeling is real to her. You should say something like "I really don't mean to treat you differently. If I do, I don't do it on purpose, and I didn't realize that I do." She might not accept it right away, but that's the first step to fixing the problem, because without this step you alienate your teen even more.

Follow through by making sure your teens know you want to spend time alone with them; it's important to them, even if they don't accept the offer. With the busy schedules that teens and their parents often have, individual attention, as little as it might happen, is something kids really appreciate. When they don't feel smothered, teens really do enjoy spending some quality time with their parents. They may not open up and tell you everything about their personal lives during your first dinner out—or ever—but remember they value being close to you and having a relationship with you, whether they say it or not.

Teens need to feel wanted, and the more often you take time together, the closer you will get to showing them that you love them just as much as your other kids. But make sure you don't guilt-trip your teen about it; don't take it personally when she just wants to hang out with friends. If you say something like "Well, I offered. I guess I know your friends are more important to you than I am," even if you're just joking around, your teen is going to take offense. We're sensitive, and when you say something like that, it's frustrating. Don't be surprised if your teen responds by lashing out at you.

Living up to Older Siblings' Standards

THIS IS ABOUT ME, NOT HER

Sixteen-year-old Hallie is sitting at the table with her mom discussing the upcoming dance at her school. Hallie is clearly excited about it, so she decides to ask her mother for a later curfew.

"Mom, the party is going to be a lot of fun and all my friends are staying out until one a.m. Is it okay if I stay out with them?"

"Not again, Hallie. We let you stay out late only a few weekends ago. Besides, your sister never asked for a later curfew, so it would be unfair to give you one."

"Yeah, exactly! She never *asked*. It's not my fault she didn't have the guts. Besides, who cares what Emily did when she was my age. This is about *me*, not *her*, so stop comparing us," shrieks Hallie at the top of her lungs as she leaves the room.

Tina, Hallie's mom, thinks Hallie is blowing this completely out of proportion, and Hallie thinks Tina is being insensitive and unfair. Not only is Hallie upset that she had her request for a later curfew turned down, she also can't stand being compared to her older sister. To you, the parent, saying "Your sister never asked" may seem like you're doing nothing more than pointing out a fact of history, but to a teenager it's the same as saying, "Why can't you be more like your sister? She's perfect." Parents should always try to avoid comparing their teens.

There *are* a few exceptions. For example, a parent does nothing wrong if she says, "Julia, you aren't allowed to have your ears pierced because you are thirteen and we made Stacey wait until she was fifteen." The reason this type of comparison is legitimate is that this is a rule you have set, based on age. It wouldn't matter if Julia was a better student, or anything else; she would still have to wait. This means it really isn't a comparison of the two children, it's just reiterating the rules of the house.

Your teenager might be upset when you state these rules, but that's something you can't avoid. You're still doing everything right. What you *can* avoid is making one of your children feel inferior, or as if she is being held to an unfair standard. You can do this by simply leaving your other children out of whatever discussion or argument you are having. It's already bad that you and your teen are fighting or disagreeing, but this is between you and her. You don't need to make it an even worse situation by bringing your other children into the conversation.

Also, remember that whenever you make a comparison, there's a good chance you will create tension between your two children.

Now, you might say to yourself, "Well, my daughter always compares herself to her older sister, saying things like 'But you let Stacey do that!' so why is it so bad for me to do the same thing?" First of all, your teen is fifteen years old and you're forty-five, and she hasn't necessarily learned yet how irrational it is to compare two entirely different people. Second, when your teen says something like that to you, it doesn't hurt your feelings (it might be annoying, but it's not hurtful), but when you compare one kid to the other, you can inadvertently hurt your teen's feelings.

If you haven't figured it out already, there are always going to be arguments between you and your teen, but there are ways to avoid turning a meaningless argument into something personal and hurtful. Comparing your teen to her older sibling is just one example. No matter what, your teen is going to be angry if she doesn't get what she wanted, like a later curfew, but you can make the best of a bad situation by avoiding sibling comparisons. Sticking to the topic at hand, and not bringing in your other kids, your teen's friends, or anybody else, will keep the fight from being blown out of proportion.

FOLLOW-UP

Now that Tina realizes Hallie was really hurt by the comparison to her older sister, she decides to go into Hallie's room to try to patch things up.

"Look, I really didn't mean to hurt you when I mentioned Emily. I shouldn't have done that. You're two different people."

"Whatever."

"Okay, you don't have to talk to me. I just want you to know that I'm sorry, and I realize what I said was unfair."

"Okay. I'm *not* talking to you."

We told you—you're going to fight and your teen is going to have an attitude. Chances are, when you make a mistake like this, your teen will milk it for all it's worth, but you're just going to have to accept it. Tina handled this well. She understood that Hallie was still angry and didn't want to talk to her, so Tina didn't push her; she understands that sometimes it's best to just let your child be, but still tell her how you feel. Hallie is trying to provoke her mom, and expects some kind of reaction when she says, "Okay, I'm *not* talking to you," so it's good Tina is being the bigger person. Hallie knows this, and that's why she made the conscious decision not to talk or accept the apology; she still wants to take advantage of her mother's mistake. The best way for a parent to deal with this is the way Tina did: leave the child alone and don't give her any more ammunition.

Battles Between Siblings

Even if you never make a mistake like that, or if you're so good at being a parent that you never do anything else to provoke things between your kids, unless your teenager is an only child, there will be conflicts. It's what siblings do, and at some point you're going to have to step in, or maybe decide it's best not to.

LIVING WITH A BULLY

James and Lily have two children, both of whom are boys. Harry, at the age of thirteen, is experiencing growth spurts for the first time and his voice is beginning to crack. Ron, Harry's older brother, finds this very amusing; so amusing that he begins calling Harry a girl.

Harry is very intimidated by Ron, the older and more popular brother, so he chooses to just take the psychological abuse.

One day James and Lily overhear Ron telling his friends about a trick he's going to play on his brother. Stunned at how malicious Ron is, James confronts Harry to confirm Ron's behavior. Afraid of being called a snitch by Ron, he denies it.

In a case like this, a parent should *never* go to the teen being bullied or intimidated. Instead you should speak with the teen who is causing problems first. This way, if the "bully" asks if you've spoken to the other sibling, no one needs to lie, and the other sibling doesn't have to deal with the consequences of being a tattletale.

No matter whom they speak to first, parents must be careful with their wording, because many things that you might say are likely to be interpreted as "You're wrong, your sister's right, your sister's my favorite child. In fact, she's perfect, and you aren't."

VIOLENCE IS NOT ACCEPTABLE

Joey is sixteen and his brother, Charlie, is twelve. The two boys are playing video games and Charlie calls Joey a douche bag. Joey punches his brother in the arm, and Charlie, in turn, kicks Joey in the back. The two boys begin to wrestle and yell out names and insults while rolling around on the floor in front of the TV.

Evan, the boys' father, comes into the den to find them wrestling, but not in a friendly or joking matter.

"Hey! Joey, get off of him! Are you crazy? You want to kill the poor kid? You're three times his size." Evan

pries Joey off of Charlie. "Joseph Smith, this is absolutely unacceptable."

"Are you kidding, Dad? What about Charlie? He
started the whole thing."

"What about him? He's twelve years old. He doesn't
know any better."

"Twelve? When I was twelve I would've been in
deep trouble for this."

"Look, Joey, you're the older brother. You need to
set an example and take some responsibility for your
actions."

"I am. I hit the little punk—I admit it—but shouldn't
he take some responsibility for calling me names and
egging me on? He's not an angel, Dad. I don't have to
take this crap from you," he yells as he walks away and
passes his smirking brother.

It was good that Evan got involved and stopped Charlie
and Joey from continuing to beat each other up; the problem
is the way he spoke to the boys after he broke up the fight. In
reality, Evan *only* spoke to Joey, and that was the reason for
Joey's outburst. He knows he shouldn't respond to name-
calling with a punch, but he feels like his father is being completely unfair.

It doesn't matter whether or not his father is right. The
way he singles out Joey in front of Charlie makes Joey feel like
he doesn't have a chance of being treated fairly. When Evan
says, "He's twelve years old. He doesn't know any better,"
Joey hears, "No matter what Charlie does, you're the one
who is going to take the blame."

On top of all this, Evan's actions also sent a message to
Charlie. By not saying anything to him, he's telling Charlie
that he can get away with anything, and Charlie will eventu-

ally abuse this, if he hasn't already. Chances are he wouldn't have provoked Joey if he didn't think he could get away with it.

This doesn't mean that your teen won't listen to what you say, it just means that you need to find a better time and setting to say it. Basically, you need to talk to each of them separately, to eliminate complicating factors, like one sibling being embarrassed or blaming the other for his actions. It's easier to get through to your kid when his brother isn't making faces at him behind your back. Plus, this way neither sibling can accuse you of not reprimanding the other one.

THE WRONG WAY TO
APPROACH CHARLIE

Evan should talk to Charlie first, because Joey was the one who was upset for being singled out. This way, when Evan does talk to Joey again, he is prepared to defend himself when Joey says, "Well, I don't see you talking to Charlie about this." Now Evan can say, "I just spoke to him, for your information."

> Evan goes into Charlie's room twenty minutes or so after the fight.
>
> "So, Charlie . . ."
>
> "Yeah, Dad?"
>
> "About that fight. I think you need to understand something."
>
> "What?"
>
> "Well, even though I didn't yell at you before, I hope you know that you're not going to just get away with whatever you want. Your mother and I are holding you responsible for all your actions. So just be aware of that."

"I know that, Dad! Who said I thought I could do whatever I want? Maybe Joey did, but he's psycho!"

"First of all, don't insult your brother. Second of all, you act like the rules don't apply to you when you plainly know that there's no fighting allowed; so you need to know that acting like you can do whatever you please isn't going to fly."

It is important to go and tell Charlie that what he did was wrong, but what Evan says in this conversation is inappropriate. Evan shouldn't be accusing Charlie of thinking he can get away with anything when Evan neglected to reprimand him just minutes before.

When Evan says, "Well, even though I didn't yell at you before, I hope you know that you're not going to just get away with whatever you want," Charlie hears, "I messed up and didn't yell at you so now I'm going to make up for my mistake by *really* yelling at you." At this point, Charlie is just going to ignore the rest and say to himself, "He's just doing this so Joey doesn't bug out at him again. I can just pretend I care and this will all go away."

THE RIGHT WAY TO APPROACH CHARLIE

Evan goes into Charlie's room twenty minutes or so after the fight.

"So, Charlie . . ."

"Yeah, Dad?"

"About that fight. I made a mistake earlier."

"Oh, yeah?"

"Well, my immediate reaction was to yell at your brother, but I realize now that both of you are responsible. Regardless of your age, you are brothers, and you need to learn how to get along civilly without me or

Tip for Sibling Squabbles

When you have these one-on-one talks, don't ask them what happened. This will only get you two different stories. Your kid probably won't be lying to you consciously, but he'll be telling it from his own slanted point of view. To find out the most truthful story, you will need to have both kids present; otherwise, one or both kids may end up manipulating you into thinking he is the victim.

Mom having to scream at either of you. What I'm trying to say is that your brother was wrong, but you were wrong today, too. Even if he started it, which I'm not saying he did, you are also responsible because you did nothing to stop the fight from happening."

"Whatever."

"Well, I won't make a big deal out of it this time, but if it happens again, there are going to be consequences."

Here, Evan got out just in time. Why? Because as far as Charlie's concerned, he was off the hook, and now he's pissed that he isn't. So, almost automatically, half of what Evan says is going to go in one ear and out the other. That's why you must keep this conversation *short and simple*. The only way you will get anywhere with this conversation is to emphasize that you hold both of them responsible, and be very direct about why fighting is a problem in your house. By doing this, your teen will at least receive the message that you think he's responsible, too, and you're not going to assign all the blame to his older brother.

THE WRONG WAY TO APPROACH JOEY

Evan goes into Joey's room twenty minutes or so after the fight.

"Joey, I shouldn't have blown up at you in front of Charlie, and I'm sorry I did that, but you also should know never to hit him."

"Either say you're sorry, or don't, Dad. Don't give me the I'm sorry *but* blah, blah, blah speech. Please leave, Dad."

Evan may as well leave at this point because anything he says is going to be blocked out after this. The second Joey heard, "I'm sorry *but*," he began to think, "My dad's just saying he's sorry to shut me up so he can go on and on about how badly I handled it all over again."

It would be best if Evan were to state the reasons Joey should never interact with his brother the way he did, and then *follow up* by saying, "and I'm really sorry for doing that in front of Charlie." If Evan says something like this, Joey will interpret it as "Dad cares about how I feel, and he was actually listening to me before."

THE RIGHT WAY TO APPROACH JOEY

Evan goes into Joey's room twenty minutes after the fight.

"So, Joey . . ."

"Yeah, Dad?"

"I've decided that I'm going to let both of you off the hook for acting the way you did—this time. You were right. I shouldn't have singled you out in front of your brother. I'm really sorry I did that. I should have waited to speak to you in private about how I feel your role in Charlie's life should be more like a role model and less of a troublemaker."

"It's not my job to set an example. That's your job, so don't throw that burden on me."

"That's not what I'm trying to say, so I'm sorry if I'm giving you that impression. What I mean is that you never had an older brother to annoy, so you don't know what it's like. He's going to annoy you constantly just because he can. Although I'll try to reprimand him for it, and get him to stop, I can't be watching him every second. Therefore, you need to try as hard as you can to ignore the squirt. I know it's really hard—believe me, I'd like to deck him every once in a while also—but you have to resist, because as a parent, when I walk in and see you punching him, I don't think about how he instigated the fight, I just see a sixteen-year-old hitting a twelve-year-old, and that doesn't look so good."

"Okay, fine. I'll try. But honestly, Dad, if he doesn't tone it down, one day I won't just be kidding when I punch him."

"And I'll try not to single you out again. Hitting isn't acceptable, so the both of you will have to work something out."

HOW TO HANDLE IT RIGHT, FROM THE START

Evan enters the den and finds Joey and Charlie fighting, and not in a friendly or joking matter.

"Are you two boys crazy?"

"He started it!" Charlie yelps.

"Yeah, right, you little schmuck. You called me a douche bag."

"And you punched me!"

"All right, all right. Give it a rest," Evan says, and shuts them both up. "You're both wrong. I thought you

Making Your Teen Feel Guilty

"Be thankful for what you have—there are children starving all over the world."

When your teen is upset, you obviously want to make her feel better, so here's a hint: if you want your teen to look on the bright side, don't say how much worse things could be. This makes her feel like what she's feeling isn't valid or it just isn't important to you. It's as if she isn't allowed to be upset about something because somewhere in the world there are worse things than what she's going through.

That may not be your aim at all, but comparing your teen's situation to a much more drastic situation isn't going to help. Looking at positive things in *her* situation is a better idea. Basically, when you say something like "Be thankful, because there are children starving all over the world, and you have it pretty good," your teen hears, "Stop being such a crybaby. What you are feeling doesn't even compare to what people with real problems are going through."

were past this immature behavior. Look, this is entirely unacceptable and I am ashamed of you both. Not only could one of you get seriously hurt, but I thought your mother and I taught you to treat each other with some respect."

"Sorry, Dad."

"Sorry, Dad."

"Sorry isn't going to cut it right now. Why don't you both cool off? We'll be talking punishment later, when your mother gets home from work."

Normally, we wouldn't encourage you to guilt-trip your kids, but in this case—when it's part of a value you want to teach your kid, and not some kind of manipulation—saying something like "I'm ashamed of you and I thought I taught you better" will go right to the heart, because it's true. You did teach your kids that violence isn't an answer to disagreements, so it's completely understandable, and it's important to reinforce that lesson when they become violent or bully one another. When they hear this, they think, "Crap, they're right. We just totally let them down."

"MOM, ALEX STOLE MY T-SHIRT."

Zoe is a sixteen-year-old sophomore in high school and her younger sister, Alex, is a fourteen-year-old freshman. The two girls often get along, but also do their fair share of bickering.

It's a Saturday evening and Alex is getting ready to go out to a party. She is in the living room when Zoe comes in.

"When did you get that shirt, Alex?" Zoe asks, somewhat suspiciously.

"I'm not sure. A long time ago," Alex responds vaguely, without looking at Zoe.

"Oh. Because it looks like this black tank top I got for my birthday last year."

"Oh . . ."

"Wait. Come over here, Alex."

"Why?"

"That *is* my tank top! I can't believe this. How long have you had it? Take it off right now."

"No, it's not!"

"Alex, I'm not stupid. That's my shirt, so take it off right now. I can't believe you actually had the nerve to hide it from me."

"I'm not hiding anything. God, you're so selfish. You won't let me borrow anything. Plus you haven't worn this in a year. You didn't even know it was missing!"

"You didn't even ask to borrow it. Basically, you just stole it. So take it off already and find something else to wear now, please."

"I'm not taking it off."

"Mom!" Zoe screams up the stairs to her mother.

"What?" her mother, Theresa, hollers back.

"Alex won't give me my shirt back!"

Their mother comes downstairs to find out what the problem is. "Alex, give her back her shirt already."

"But, Mom—"

"Don't 'but Mom' me. This is a ridiculous conversation, and I don't really want to have it. You're both being immature. Just give her back her shirt, Alex. Otherwise, she won't leave you alone. You know Zoe's very picky about her stuff."

"Excuse me," Zoe butts in. "The girl stole my shirt and now *I'm* to blame because I'm picky?"

"This isn't even any of Mom's business, so I don't know why you called her down here," Alex yells at her sister.

"Because you're such a baby you need an adult to make you do the right thing."

"All right, girls, that's enough. Both of you to your rooms. This is absurd."

This fight was totally unnecessary and could have been completely prevented. No, the first request to take off the shirt and any stubbornness that follows is not something you could have prevented. Your kids are going to fight, but the level to which the fight escalates could have been controlled a lot better.

Because the mother got involved, the fight went in a totally different direction and then got out of hand. To avoid this sort of result, the best thing you can do as a parent is stay out of your kids' business when it comes to things like this. When your kids are bickering about an article of clothing, or whose turn it is for the bathroom or the computer, a parent getting involved really isn't going to solve the situation. Even if you come up with a good compromise, nobody is going to be happy.

When you get involved, it's hard not to sound like you're favoring one kid, or saying one kid is right and one is wrong. Therefore, when the situation really isn't urgent or unsafe, it's best not to get involved.

For example, when Theresa says, "You know Zoe's very picky about her stuff," Zoe hears, "Even though your sister took your shirt without asking, you're to blame because you're not willing to share and you're a bad sister." When Theresa says, "Alex, give her back her shirt already," Alex hears, "Don't be immature. You're always making things so difficult." Neither girl is happy with how this all turned out once their mother got involved.

Also, you may end up getting frustrated just like Theresa does, and then do something like punish your kids or send them to their rooms because they're getting on your nerves. This is not good. It all started as a conversation about a tank top or some other trivial thing, and now they're getting punished. There was no need for the situation to reach such extremes.

Instead of getting involved, let the situation play out. It will get resolved somehow. Even though Alex and Zoe may not be acting mature, they both know it's ridiculous to fight over a shirt; eventually they'll get tired of fighting and one of them will give in.

Tips for the Future

Spend time with your kids individually.

Compliment *each* of your kids on qualities that are specific to them.

Show them that you care. If they think you are favoring one sibling, show them that you want to change this perception. Don't just insist that you don't; say something like "I don't, but clearly I've been doing something wrong for you to think that. Help me out. Tell me what I've done so I can change things and you can tell that I love you both equally."

A BETTER WAY TO HANDLE
THE SITUATION

"Mom!" Zoe calls for her mother. "Alex won't give me my shirt back!"

Theresa comes halfway down the stairs.

"Zoe, Alex, I'm not getting involved in this. I think you two can work out your differences over a shirt without me. Isn't that right?"

It's as simple as that. We're not saying that you should ignore your kids whenever they ask you to get involved, but when it's a situation like this, you can just tell them you don't want to get involved and they'll understand. Your teens won't get mad at you for not joining in, because they know there's no real reason for you to get involved.

Friends

Trying to Choose Your Teen's Friends

Every parent tries to be protective. The thing is, no matter how reasonable you try to be about it, we teens are going to think you are being overprotective if you don't just agree with us. One of the places this is going to show up a lot is when it comes to friends. Just like with curfews and other privileges, we're going to be fighting for more freedom, while you think you're just trying to look out for us.

You used to have a lot of influence on who our friends were; if you go back far enough, you were actually picking them out and making playdates, but even after that you knew our friends' parents and you could talk to them about what was going on. By the time we're teenagers, though, we're meeting other teens that you've never met, and you're probably not going to meet their parents, either. They might not be from our neighborhood, or go to our school, and they might look or act like somebody you really don't want us to know.

Unfortunately, sorry to say, when it comes to this, your opinion doesn't count. When you say to a kid, "Don't be friends with him" or "I don't want you to hang out with him anymore," it's just the same as saying, "Don't look in that box." In your kid's head this is directly translated as "Quick, look in that box, before Mom comes back." Some teens will assume that their parents are embellishing the reasons why they should not hang out with a particular person, out of overprotectiveness, and some teens find the other kid appealing for exactly the same reasons you don't want them to be friends.

The truth is that no kid will listen to you about their friends; you think they need to hear your reasons, but if your child is not in the right mind-set, then whatever you say will go in one ear and out the other. If you are really determined to have some say in who their friends are, you're going to have to use a very subtle approach.

Another issue you may find yourself dealing with is getting to know your teen's friends to begin with. Your teen is not going to make it easy for you to do this, but there are still ways for you to get to know them without becoming a really annoying and overbearing parent. Or too much, anyway.

Part of being a successful parent is understanding that in the end, you can't pick your teen's friends. Although you can attempt to have some influence, at some point you need to draw the line and allow teens to make their own decisions.

"YOU CAN'T HANG OUT WITH THEM ANYMORE!"

Will is fifteen years old, and a freshman in high school. Recently, he has been mentioning some new friends, and his father, Spencer, is worried that he is no longer hanging out with the same reliable boys who had been his friends since kindergarten. So when Will comes into his father's room to tell him his plans for the night, which include his new friends Ted and Chris, Spencer takes the opportunity to talk to Will about how he feels they might not be so good for his son.

"You know, Will, I wanted to talk to you about Ted and Chris."

"About what?"

"Well, I just get a bad vibe from them."

"You've got to be kidding. You've met them *once*. How could you even get any vibe from them?"

"I know, but they don't seem like the good guys you used to hang out with, like Samuel and Albert. They came from good homes and they were always respectful. These new boys didn't even say 'hi' to me when I came into your room. You know, son, if you lie down with the pigs, you come up smelling like them."

"What are you talking about? You're babbling about farm animals now."

"I'm just saying that maybe you shouldn't hang out with them so much. I don't want you in with the wrong crowd. You're starting high school. You need friends that you can depend on. These two punks look like friends you can depend on for drugs or something, not for support."

"I honestly can't believe one word that's coming out of your mouth right now. It's disgusting. You don't even know them! Do you really think you can classify my friends from the way they wear their pants or something? They're my friends, and I'm going to keep hanging out with them, so give it a rest!"

"You won't be seeing them as long as I have anything to do with it! I've heard about these boys from other parents, and the word is that they are bad news."

"You've been checking up on my friends? I do not believe this! I'm fifteen! You can't keep trying to make my decisions for me! I can't stand it anymore!" shrieks Will.

Spencer's attempt to influence his son's choice of friends went badly because of how he approached the situation. Spencer was thinking he could tell Will whom to hang out with and whom to avoid, but as you probably realize now, your teen doesn't want to hear your opinion on this subject.

There are a variety of reasons that Will could be hanging out with Chris and Ted, but the main one is probably that he thinks they're cool, and he's having fun with them. With this in mind, it does not make sense for Spencer to insult these new friends if he's trying to get Will to stop hanging out with them.

When Spencer says, "These two punks look like friends you can depend on for drugs or something, not for support," Will is going to be completely and utterly insulted. What he hears is "You can't even manage to choose appropriate friends, and rather than try to understand why you like these kids, I'm going to insult them and therefore insult you." When Spencer makes the comment about talking to other parents, to Will it's like he's driving that same point home. Will hears, "I don't trust your decisions and I have my spies watching you and your friends."

There are only two possibilities. Either your teen believes these kids are nice, so why *wouldn't* he be friends with them? Or he knows his new friends aren't the best kids on the block, but when you insult them or say he's falling in with the wrong crowd or—worst of all—forbid him to see them, it will just fuel his desire to hang out with them.

Either way, putting your foot down and saying, "I'm an adult and I know that these kids are going to be bad in the long run, so you can't hang out with them," is just not going to work. In fact, it's going to work against you, and maybe cause the opposite of what you want. By putting this kind of strain on your relationship with your teen, you will push him away and make him even less likely to listen to your advice.

Unfortunately, this is one of those areas where teenagers have to learn for themselves. Your teen has to realize that these kids aren't people he wants to be hanging out with (if that's even the case—remember, you could be wrong about them). The trick is how to help a teenager see this without pushing him away, and without waiting until the situation gets so bad that he learns the hard way (gets arrested, gets hurt, etc.).

"YOU MAY NOT WANT TO HEAR THIS, BUT . . ."

Spencer is frustrated with Will's decision to hang out with Ted and Chris. He finally realizes that the only way he can get Will to understand that these kids are bad news is if he realizes it on his own. At one point in Spencer's life he had a friend, Barry, who didn't really treat him well, and Ted's manners and disregard for the rules remind him a lot of that friend. Spencer decides to talk to Will about Barry, and try to get him to see a parallel between Ted and his friend.

> After he finishes telling the story, he ends by saying, "So now do you see why I have such a problem with Ted? He's bad news. Listen to someone who has experienced it and knows better."

We strongly encourage parents to draw parallels between their own lives and their teens' in order to reinforce a rule or a point. Although times have changed, and your teen will be the first to point that out, issues like respect and choosing good friends are timeless. The problem is, Spencer can't finish up by saying something like "So now do you see why I don't like Ted?" Will hears this as "I am going to talk down to you now because it makes me feel like I still have power as a parent," instead of "I'm trying to protect you from getting hurt."

A parent doesn't want to come off as condescending—"I told you so"—because that will only lead to more fights and less progress. If Spencer had left out the last part, and just talked about his own experience, Will might have taken something valuable away from the conversation.

Even if your teen responds to a story from your own experience by dismissing you with an "Okay, whatever," you shouldn't shove the parallel in his face. He gets it. That "whatever" is just to make sure nobody thinks he's giving in and seeing things your way. No teen wants to admit when a parent might be onto something wise.

Remember, even if your child doesn't sever all ties with his "Ted," your story will stay in the back of his mind, and he'll remember it when his friend acts in the way you predicted. Eventually, that story may keep your teen out of trouble.

If you don't have an experience that is similar to your kid's, *do not make one up.* What goes around comes around. If you lie, your teen will find out, and you can't be surprised when he starts lying to you.

Instead, here's an alternative approach.

"WHY DO YOU HANG OUT WITH THAT DOPE ANYWAY?"

Spencer has this bad feeling about Ted and Chris and decides it's time to talk about it with Will.

"Will, do you have a minute to talk?"

"Yeah, sure. What?" Will turns away from his computer.

"I just wanted to talk about Ted and the other guys."

"What do you mean?"

"Well, you've been spending a lot of time with them recently and I just wanted to hear about what they're like."

"I don't know. What do you want me to say?"

"I know it sounds weird, but I used to know all your friends, when you were hanging out with Samuel and them. Now that you're getting older, and I don't always know your friends directly, I'd just like to know a little bit about them. I mean, you like hanging out with them so there must be some reason that it's them and not Joe Schmo."

"Well, I don't know. Uhh . . . Ted's funny and stuff."

"What's he into in school?"

"Dad, I don't talk to Ted about that stuff."

"Okay. Well, what are his parents like?"

"What is this, Twenty Questions?"

"Sorry, I know it must feel like I'm grilling you, but I just want to know a little bit about these guys if you're going to be out with them until all hours of the night. I can't be there to control you when you're out with your friends. I understand that, so I just want to make sure you're hanging out with good guys. I trust your instincts, but I'm your dad, and it's my job to talk to you about this stuff because I care about you."

"Okay, Dad, don't get all sentimental on me. Look, they're good guys. I feel comfortable hanging out with them, so you should too, okay? I know when a scene is sketchy and I can watch out for myself. Okay?"

"I know that."

Even though it might seem like Spencer is prying when he asks his son about Ted, that's not the case. He's being respectful (not saying "Why do you hang out with these schmucks?") and giving Will an incentive to tell him about the friend. Spencer gives Will an explanation that makes Will comfortable enough to share information, because he doesn't feel like it's an interrogation, but rather, sincere curiosity (". . . so now that you're getting older and I don't always know your friends directly, I'd just like to know a little bit about them"); he can sense that Spencer is just doing what dads are supposed to do. If Spencer hadn't given Will a good explanation, Will would probably be thinking, "My dad's such a control freak; he wants to know about everything in my life. Why can't he just butt out?"

When Spencer says, "You like hanging out with them, so there must be some reason that it's them and not Joe Schmo," Will can understand where his dad's curiosity is coming from. Spencer doesn't give Will a reason to think, "My dad hates my friends and won't give them a chance."

If you're in a situation like this with your teen, you should also be aware that his old friends might not be the best possible friends anymore, or might not even be possible friends anymore. Old friends aren't always good friends. You have to remember that kids in ninth grade are different than they were in fourth grade, and maybe your teen's old friends aren't the same as they used to be, or aren't the same with your teen.

There's always the possibility that your teen knows that these friends are not role-model quality, but they're the ones who accept him and give him a place to sit at lunchtime. His old friends might have become part of a different social group, and your teen doesn't fit into it, or doesn't want to. Maybe the new friends that don't seem like good choices to you are the only kids who are willing to accept your teen now, or they're the ones that make him feel like he belongs. So before you go trying to make him switch friends, keep in mind that the ones that seem less than perfect to you might be his only option.

Spencer, by posing the questions about Ted and why Will likes him, forces Will to evaluate Ted. By the end of the discussion, Will may have, with Spencer's indirect help, figured out that this friend isn't such a great friend after all. This doesn't mean that he's going to stop hanging out with Ted right away, because it's just not that easy in high school, but it may put things in perspective for him. This is not to say that if your teen is changing (for the worse) that his new friends haven't been a contributing factor; it just means that your kid can stay the same even if he's not hanging out with the cream of the crop, because he may know they aren't the best.

"FAMILIARITY BREEDS CONTEMPT."

Buffy has a fourteen-year-old daughter named Lana. Buffy's best friend, Skylar, also has a fourteen-year-old daughter, Emika, at the same school as Lana. Emika and

Lana are not friends even though their mothers are.
Buffy feels like Lana could learn a lot from Emika, who
loves to read poetry, among other things. Buffy decides
to take it upon herself to make a dinner reservation for
the four of them.

"I made dinner plans for us and Emika and Skylar for
next week."

"Why?"

"What do you mean 'Why?' Because I think it will be
nice, and I think that you guys should get to know each
other better. Skylar is such a great person, I'm sure you'll
feel the same way about her daughter, since she's like a
younger version of Skylar."

"First of all, she's not a younger version of Skylar. I
don't know where you get that idea. I go to school with
Emika, I know her much better!" Lana screams at her
mother. "Second of all, I don't want to have dinner with
them; there's a reason I'm not friends with her. So have a
nice dinner, because I'm not coming."

"You're not even giving her a chance."

"Don't you think we'd already be friends if we
wanted to be? Don't you get it? There's no point in
having dinner, because we don't have anything to say to
each other. You can't control who my friends are!"

"Well, I've already made the plans, so you don't
really have a choice. It would look really bad if we can-
celed. And you know what? It offends me that you don't
even attempt to be friends with her, because I'm good
friends with Skylar."

"Well, it offends me that you could make these
plans without checking with me. Honestly, you chose
not to ask me, so you got yourself into this mess and

you can get yourself out of it. It's not my responsibility and I don't have to do what I don't want to."

"Well then, I'll remember that the next time you need me to do something for you."

Of course, *many* things went wrong in this conversation, but the main problem is that Lana feels like her mother is trying to get too involved in her life. Basically, Buffy shouldn't be making plans without consulting her teenager. More importantly, she shouldn't be trying to choose Lana's friends along the way. It's just as bad to try to force teens to be friends with someone as it is to try to keep them from being friends with someone.

When Buffy says, "You're not even giving her a chance," even though she doesn't say it, Lana is thinking, "You think you know everything!" Lana is annoyed because she was never even asked if she wanted to go, and now she is being accused of not giving the girl a chance, when she feels like Buffy didn't give *her* a chance to explain why dinner was a bad idea to begin with.

Also, Buffy shouldn't have assumed that Emika would be just like Skylar and then go a step further, assuming that Lana would therefore like Emika. Lana hears, "I have no idea and don't care what you value in a friendship, or even what kind of person you like to hang out with."

The worst thing Buffy does is say, "I'll remember that the next time you need me to do something for you." Using guilt is never a good idea and will always end up working against you. In fact, Lana probably thinks Buffy is acting like a ten-year-old and is that much less likely to listen to what she has to say.

GETTING TO KNOW YOUR
TEEN'S FRIENDS

If you are feeling so much apprehension about the people your son or daughter is hanging out with that you're trying to arrange for them to have different friends, it's probably because you don't really know their friends. That can be scary. That's why it's important to try to get to know your teen's friends. Although your teen can make this difficult, it's really important. In the end, your teen will probably be happy you know her friends because she'll know you trust her to be with them. In fact, during this process you may end up learning a lot about your teen you never knew.

You're dying to know what's going on in your teen's life and you're also dying to get to know your teen's friends. How will you ever be able to do that without becoming the crazy, nosy, overbearing parent? Well, one way is to offer to take your teen and some friends out to dinner with you one night, or to an event like a basketball game. The reason he might accept the invitation is because he likes a good meal and he knows his allowance won't get him one as good as the one you're offering, or he knows that he can't afford to go to the game without you.

All you have to do is say, "I'll behave myself in front of your friends and it's a free meal. Come on, what's not to like?" This will be the perfect opportunity to get your kid to open up, because your teen's friends will usually start to talk, and that will get your own teen to loosen up a little. (Believe us, this will work better than asking, "What did you do in school today?" every day, and being told "Nothing" every time, even though it's never the truth.) Eventually you'll be having a conversation you never expected.

It might be best to keep it to only one or two friends; otherwise it could become a night about the teens. You get left out of the conversation completely, and your only function is to pick up the check.

When You're Out with *Your* Friends: Manners for Teens

All parents want their teens to be perfectly well mannered and pleasant to be around, especially when they're out with other people. Realistically, this isn't going to happen. Instead, your teen is probably going to have a stain on his shirt before you go to dinner, and will be flossing his teeth at the dinner table fifteen minutes after you've sat down. He might not always be pleasant to people who call your house or friends you introduce him to. Basically, you can teach your teen good manners but he still may not act like a perfect gentleman. In fact, he may go out of his way not to, and floss his teeth in the middle of a play just to rub you the wrong way.

"SIT UP STRAIGHT. YOU LOOK LIKE THE HUNCHBACK OF NÔTRE-DAME."

It's a Friday night and the Stewarts have decided to go out for a nice dinner with family friends. Fourteen-year-old Kelly is slouched over the table, pushing her mashed potatoes back and forth on the plate. When a question is addressed to her, she gives a one-word response and talks down at her plate so no one can really understand what she's saying.

"Sit up," says Kelly's mother, Alice.

"What?"

"You heard me. Sit up. You're slouching. Think about where you are. This is a nice restaurant."

"Like I didn't know that already?"

"Don't be a wiseass, Kelly."

"Whatever you say, Mom," mumbles Kelly sarcastically.

"Hmnashiv drteslash," Alice says.

"What?"

"That's what you sound like. I can't understand a word
you say. Try speaking up instead of down into your plate."

"Why don't *you* try minding your own business for
once?"

If you really want to create a scene in the restaurant, then
feel free to mock your kid. If you don't, then we suggest you
stay away from things like that. (Refer to "When Teasing
Your Teen Becomes Hurtful" in chapter 1 to get a better sense
of when it's okay to poke a little fun at your teen and when
it's crossing the line.)

It seems pretty typical for parents to say something like
"We're in a restaurant. Sit up," or "We're guests in someone's
home. Don't touch that." When you say something like that,
though, all you are doing is stating the obvious. You aren't enlightening your kid by reminding her of her surroundings; all
you are doing is bugging her and making her want to lunge
toward you, which probably isn't a great idea, especially since
you're in a restaurant, or someone's home.

Frankly, your teen isn't going to take any criticism well if
it's in a public place. It doesn't matter how close you are to
the friends you are with, your teen will see your comments as
a way to embarrass her instead of as a reasonable attempt to
correct her manners. When you remind your teen to have
better manners, you're probably thinking that you're doing
her a favor by saving her the embarrassment of looking like a
slob in public, but from your teen's point of view *you* are the
main cause of her embarrassment.

The whole purpose of the conversation, or in this case,

Alice's series of demands, was to correct Kelly's behavior. Instead she just got lip from her daughter and no improvement in the manners department.

A BETTER APPROACH

The Stewarts are out to dinner with friends.

"Kelly, try not to slouch," her mother calmly whispers.

"I'm not slouching." Kelly tries to straighten her back slowly, so as not to make it obvious to her mother that she's doing what she wants.

"Okay. It's a nice restaurant. I just wanted to remind you."

"Like I didn't know that already?"

"Okay, okay."

This conversation may not seem *that* much better to you, but it really is. Your teen isn't going to automatically do what you say, and she isn't going to want to acknowledge when you are right (like we've said many times before), but your teen can hear you when you comment on something minor and say something like "Try not to slouch." If you say it in a respectful voice—asking, rather than ordering her around—your teen will probably sit up after a minute or two, even though she doesn't say, "Oh, you're right, Mom!"

What makes this conversation much better than the first is how Kelly's mother reacts to Kelly's response. This time, the mother just lets Kelly be, instead of leaning on her harder. She knows that it's neither the time nor place to get into a fight, and the way to prevent a fight over such a trivial matter is to be the bigger person and drop the subject. Plus, she probably noticed that Kelly realized she was slouching and sat up.

Chapter 5

"I Want You to Express Yourself, but Take That Shirt Off!":

Clothing, Tattoos and Piercing

When your child's self-expression takes the form of body piercing, or clothing that you think is inappropriate, you're dealing with more than just fashion; issues of self-esteem and confidence are always involved, too. As you've all surely figured out, teens are demanding and also very sensitive, and most of us are trying to restrain ourselves from blaming you for everything that goes wrong in our lives. Even so, parents should not be forced to tiptoe around their teenager making sure not to upset him.

Although teens and parents have different opinions about what kinds of clothing are acceptable (e.g., kids see below-the-hip-bone jeans as normal, and parents can't believe teens think the waist is five inches below where it really is), teens will sometimes appreciate your interference when revealing clothes make them a target for harassment or worse just by walking down the street. Although it's true that some teenagers crave attention, no teen would feel comfortable if faced with a situation like that. If you just explain to a girl

that *she*, not you, won't feel comfortable in a particular outfit, she might appreciate the advice and change, even if she
goes through the motions of fighting with you about it.

Another problem your teen's wardrobe might present is if
he wears something offensive, such as a T-shirt with a racial
or religious slur printed on it. Once again, this is your cue to
get involved; explain to your teen that although this may be
how he is choosing to express himself, some may find the ap-
parel insulting.

We said that your teens might appreciate your advice, but
if they don't, things can get a lot stickier. When it comes to you
facing your daughter and telling her to "take off that shirt because your chest is exposed," you are entering a whole other
realm. In high school and middle school, there are very distinct
social groups, and most kids are going to want to be part of
one of them; for teenagers, this is a big part of "who you are."
In order to be a part of a social group, one must dress a certain
way. Dress is often the trademark for who is "cool" and who is
not. When you ask your teenager to change her shirt, you think
you're talking about clothing, but to your teenager, you could
be asking her to give up her claim to being cool and belonging.

Dress Code

When Your Teen Is Wearing Extremely Inappropriate Clothing (Inappropriate by *Your* Standards at Least)

"THAT SHIRT MAKES YOU LOOK LIKE A SLUT!"

Simon's daughter Judy doesn't see the way she looks
in her clothing. Her body has begun maturing and she

may not understand that the way she looks in her head is different from the way others see her.

Recently, Britney Spears has fallen out of favor in Judy's social group. Simon knows he can use that as leverage.

"Are you really going to wear that today?" Simon asks Judy as she comes into the kitchen wearing a low-cut shirt.

"Why else would I have it on?"

"Well, Britney wears that type of shirt and everyone calls her a slut because of it. You don't want to be called a slut like that, do you?"

"Yeah, that's *exactly* what I want," Judy yells sarcastically as she storms past Simon.

No, he didn't just say that. No, no, no, Simon. It's a *good* idea to point out that Britney owns a shirt like that, but it's not a good idea to tell your daughter, "Hey, you look like a slut." You have to let your teen draw her own conclusions when you point out that you've seen Britney wearing something similar. If you don't let her figure it out for herself, you become the enemy, *plus* she won't change the shirt.

When Simon says, "Are you really going to wear that?" he's asking for a snotty response because she's clearly planning to wear the outfit, otherwise she wouldn't have it on. Same thing when Simon says, "You don't want to be called a slut like that, do you?" He's just begging for a sarcastic response.

Judy's probably so pissed off that even if she had intended to change the shirt before, she won't now, because she thinks that would be sending the message that her father is right and that she cares about his opinion.

What Simon wants to do instead is *casually* point out to Judy what's going on; he can do this just by saying, "Judy, I saw Britney wearing that in a magazine." You'd be surprised what that can do to a girl at the age of fourteen. Within seconds, the shirt will be put away, without Simon having to look like the bad guy.

Note: This strategy can work on boys too, but clearly you'll have to use a male celebrity.

"WHY DON'T YOU TRY ON THE BLUE SHIRT? IT'S A LITTLE MORE FLATTERING."

Edna is getting dressed for her friend's birthday party and decides to put on a pink shirt that is too tight for her. Lillian, her mother, takes notice of this and decides she wants to tell Edna about the top to save her from embarrassment.

"Let me see how the outfit looks," says Lillian.

Edna twirls around, looking confident.

"Maybe you should wear something else. . . ."

"Why?"

"Well, you have more flattering things to wear, that's all."

"That's your opinion," says Edna, with an edge to her voice.

"Okay. This doesn't look good on you, in my opinion."

"Okay, then don't look at it," says Edna as she turns back toward the mirror.

Lillian starts the conversation off well by coming in and casually asking to see the outfit. This is good because Lillian is taking the time to help Edna, which shows Edna that she actually cares, which is the most important thing. Your teen needs to understand that you *do* care, and you aren't just say-ing it doesn't look good because you want her to feel bad about herself.

Just like in the last situation, though, word choice is very important here. When it comes to body image, you need to be especially delicate.

When Lillian says things like "Maybe you should wear something else" and "You have more flattering things to wear," she is digging herself into a serious hole with Edna. Edna interprets these comments as "You look fat" or "You look like a hooker," depending on which insecurity she's feel-ing most on that particular day.

If you say anything like that, your teen will automatically become really defensive, like Edna. No teen is going to stand around while she is being insulted. Instead the teen is going to turn it around and make it clear that the parent is in fact the stupid and uninformed one.

You may be thinking, "Okay, no harm done. So what if she insults me back?" Well, wrong. Much harm has been done. Parents have to *really* try to understand that teens do hold grudges and rarely forget when a parent says something as hurtful as "That doesn't look good on you." To the teen, you aren't just referring to the outfit when you say this, you are saying that her body is flawed.

FOLLOW-UP: HOW TO UNDO THE DAMAGE BEFORE IT'S TOO LATE

Lillian realizes that what she said to Edna may have hurt her feelings. After a half hour has passed, she de-cides that she should try to talk things out with Edna, so there's no misunderstanding about what she meant.

"Edna, listen . . ."

"No, thanks. I think I've heard enough from you tonight."

"I'm sorry."

"Whatever. Clearly you don't think this shirt is meant for my body. Why would you say you're sorry? You don't mean it."

"I'm afraid that what I said earlier was misleading. I didn't mean to say I thought the shirt was ugly on you, it's just that I think you have so many other great options for shirts to wear that I hate to see you wear that one. There are other shirts that are much more flattering, like the blue or brown shirts, and I know you want to look your best, so I thought I was being helpful by telling you my opinion. Instead I wasn't, and I made you feel bad in the process, so I'm sorry."

"Well, it's too late now. Now, can you please leave me alone before you say something else that you don't mean."

"Please just think about what I'm saying."

You don't want to force this conversation on your teen. Chances are she is really hurt, and she's being so snappy with you because she doesn't want to start crying. It's easier for a teen to be angry and sullen than to be honest and cry in front of you. Frankly, we find it embarrassing to cry in front of you guys, especially when it was you who made the hurtful comments to begin with. We wouldn't want to make it obvious that your comment meant so much.

It was good of Lillian to start off her explanation by saying she phrased her comment badly. This shows that Lillian is willing to take responsibility for offending her daughter instead of trying to take either half credit or no credit. By saying, "I'm afraid that what I said earlier was misleading," Lillian is acknowledging that her comment was hurtful and she understands why, but she also wants Edna to know that she didn't intend it to come out that way, even though it did. Lillian even took it a step further, when she didn't have to, by saying exactly what she meant to say.

Also, if you're in a situation like this, you should know that it's not helpful for a parent to say, "You have other flattering things," if you aren't going to give examples. Chances are your teen was trying on outfits for at least a half hour and couldn't find a better option. She must have thought the shirt she was wearing was the best choice, because she's wearing it, so if you don't have a specific example, your advice is not only worthless, it makes the situation even more frustrating for your teen.

A BETTER APPROACH
"Let me see how the outfit looks," says Lillian.
Edna twirls around looking confident.
"I like it, but I like the blue or purple shirt better."
"Really? Why?"
"Not sure. It's just my taste. I think the other shirts flatter your body more."

TIP
Stay away from phrases like "Stop being so sensitive" *whether your teen is overreacting or not.* It will never help the situation. It will only make your teen feel worse than she already does.

"Hmmm. Okay. I'll see," says Edna as she turns back toward the mirror to get a second, more critical look at the outfit.

When you are dealing with body image, you want to keep your conversations short, simple, and direct—this way there is no room for misinterpretation. In the conversation above,

Dress Code for Parents

Just like you become embarrassed when your teen wears certain clothing, your teenager is sometimes embarrassed when you wear clothing that is considered "young for your age." Clearly, you are entitled to wear whatever you want, and your teen can't stop you, but keep in mind that if you are going to criticize certain things that we wear, we will feel entitled to insult what you wear.

Try to stay away from trends that are marketed for teens if you think your teen might be sensitive to the way you dress. Teens want and need to have boundaries between themselves and their parents, so the way parents dress can become a very sensitive issue. The last thing you want to do is borrow your daughter's or son's clothes. Not only will the simple fact that you're wearing their clothes be mortifying, but if they look "better" on you, well, let's not even talk about it. It's better for everyone involved if we never find out, okay?

Lillian was smart to say, "I like it, but I like the blue or purple shirt better." This is pretty direct. It's telling Edna she has better options and what they are, so Edna doesn't have to start looking for a new outfit all over again.

Also, When Edna asks why she likes the other shirts better, it was good for Lillian to say, "It's just my taste." This way, if Edna decides to wear the shirt she already has on, it's just because she has a different idea of what looks good and what doesn't, not because she's trying to make a statement to her mom.

"YOU WILL COVER YOUR ENTIRE BUTT WHEN WE GO TO GRANDMA'S."

It's eleven a.m. and the Schuel family is running late. They were supposed to be at their grandparents' house for brunch already. Carol and Harvey are waiting in the foyer for their fifteen-year-old son, Jason. After they scream for him for ten minutes, he slugs out of his room in his ripped sweatpants (which he obviously slept in). Harvey is pissed off. All this time he's been waiting, Jason wasn't even getting ready, he was catching up on more sleep.

"Are you kidding? You're not wearing that out of the house!" screams Harvey. *"Go back in your room and change immediately. We are already late because of you!"*

"Whoa, take a chill pill, Dad. What's your problem? We aren't going anyplace fancy. It's just Grandma's house. I want to wear my sweatpants, so that's what I'm going to wear."

"You can wear your sweatpants, but then you aren't coming."

"Okay with me, psycho."

We understand that it's frustrating to be late because of your teen. We also know that it's inconsiderate, but really, that doesn't mean we care. If it isn't important to us—and clearly, being on time to Grandma's house isn't important to Jason—then it takes a lot of effort to motivate us to do something, let alone do it on time.

It's pretty obvious Harvey knows all this; this isn't the first time. That's why he's so angry when Jason walks in like nothing is the matter, but getting angry isn't going to help the situation—it's only going to make it worse. First of all, your teen is going to have an attitude whenever he wakes up in the morning, no matter how much sleep he got, so as the parent, you need to decide if you really want to discuss the issue of tardiness this early (early for your teen, anyway). It might not be in anyone's best interest. After all, you have an hour's drive to Grandma's, and your son knows just how to make a car ride incredibly unpleasant. You might want to hold off on the actual discussion of what's unacceptable until after Grandma's.

When Harvey starts screaming, Jason doesn't think, "Oh. Maybe my sweatpants are a little inappropriate after all. I better go back and change before I make Dad even angrier." What he thinks is, "What a pain in the ass. He obviously didn't get enough sleep last night," because to Jason, this just isn't a big deal, so there must be some other reason his father is acting like this.

Frankly, Jason thinks his reasoning is pretty solid. They aren't going anyplace fancy and he sees no reason why sweatpants shouldn't be acceptable. So, when Harvey responds with what Jason hears as an ultimatum—change or don't come—Jason accepts the challenge and opts not to come.

Of course you don't want to ignore the issue completely. But Harvey could have just said something like "You realize we're going to be late now because of you, right?" That's enough to send the message loud and clear.

Honestly, the first thing you need to ask yourself as a parent before you get into any argument is, "Is this issue important enough to get into a fight about?" Every parent needs to pick and choose his battles; if you don't, then your kid is going to stop being able to differentiate between things he really needs to listen to you about and things that aren't that big a deal. If there's a fight about a new issue every day, he's going to stop taking you seriously—which is the worst thing that could possibly happen.

If the sweatpants really are a big deal to you, then look below for a better approach. If sweatpants aren't really that important but you want him to know you'd prefer a different outfit, then say, "Listen, I'm not going to ask you to change now because we are already running late, but next time we go to your grandmother's, can you try to wear something a little less casual? I think she'd appreciate it." That should do the trick. Maybe he'll wear the gross sweatpants this time, but now you only have one issue to battle about—"inconsiderate tardiness"—which is probably more important than the sweatpants issue.

A BETTER APPROACH

"Jason, can you please change your sweatpants?"

"Um . . . why?"

"I know we are just going to Grandma's house, but I think she might find the sweatpants disrespectful."

"That's her problem. I find her old-people breath disgusting, but I don't tell her to brush her teeth, do I?"

"Don't be a wiseass. Just do me a favor and change

into some jeans, and not the ones that hang below your ass."

"Fine," snaps Jason while rolling his eyes.

"Thanks, pal, and hurry up while you're at it. Since you decided to sleep an extra twenty minutes, we are going to be late."

"Oops."

This is a pretty successful exchange. Even though Harvey is pissed off that Jason has kept them waiting, he's managed to stay calm and just slip in a casual remark on the subject. This is good because he's now made Jason aware of it, and he can really address the matter later.

Also, it's good that Harvey doesn't snap at Jason when Jason is a wiseass and makes a rude remark regarding Harvey's mom. Instead, he tells him lightly to shut his mouth and do him a favor. This way Harvey isn't really demanding anything; it's more like he's pretending to ask Jason. Jason can't take offense at "Just do me the favor and change," because Harvey phrased it so that it was Jason's choice.

When Your Teen Is Wearing Something Extremely Offensive

"THAT SHIRT MAKES YOU LOOK LIKE A RACIST!": THE APPROACH TO AVOID, EVEN IF IT'S UNAVOIDABLE

Recently Ted has taken a liking to a new cartoon show on Comedy Central. He likes it so much that he's begun wearing T-shirts with quotes from the show. The most recent shirt he added to his collection features a phrase that could be taken out of context as racist. His

father, Andrew, is worried that if Ted wears this to
school or on the subway, he might be confronted by
people who find the shirt insulting. Trying to protect his
son and watch out for his safety, Andrew talks to Ted
about the T-shirt.

Ted walks into the kitchen to say good-bye before
leaving for school.

"Are you out of your mind wearing that shirt to
school?"

"What? Why?"

"*Why?* You are asking to get decked if you wear it."

"Again. Why?" says Ted, with an attitude.

"Did it not dawn on you that someone might be offended by the comment on that T-shirt?"

"So what? Then they shouldn't look."

"You've gotta be kidding me. You think if someone
said something that offended you, you would just keep
walking and ignore it? No, you'd smack him. If you know
what's best for you, you'll listen to me and go change
your shirt."

"Gee, thanks for the advice," snaps Ted sarcastically,
as he turns toward the front door.

Andrew has the right idea. He just lets his anger get in the
way of what was really a pretty logical explanation of why Ted
shouldn't wear an offensive shirt. Andrew makes a strong
case when he says, "You think if someone said something that
offended you, you would just keep walking and ignore it?"
Most teenage boys are pretty confrontational, and chances
are that they wouldn't walk away from something that offended them. Ted probably gets it.

The problem is that Andrew sandwiched an important

point between comments like "You've gotta be kidding me" and "If you know what's best for you, you'll listen to me." You have no shot of getting through to your kid if you start out by making him feel stupid, or say something that makes him feel like you think you're always right and he's always wrong.

"YOUR SHIRT MIGHT OFFEND SOMEONE.": THE SUCCESSFUL APPROACH

Ted walks into the kitchen to say good-bye before leaving for school.

"I was thinking. . . . You might want to reconsider wearing that shirt to school," Andrew says.

"Um . . . why?"

"Well, some people might get offended by it. I'm not saying you need to be sensitive to everyone's feelings, but the last thing you want is trouble. . . ."

"I don't think anyone's going to bother me over a T-shirt. That's pretty pathetic," says Ted with an attitude.

"I agree, but pathetic or not, it's highly possible. If a shirt offended you, can you confidently say you'd walk away without at least making a comment?"

"Yep."

"All right. You don't have to change. It was just a suggestion. I know that I would deck someone if they were wearing something that really offended me."

"Just drop it, okay? I'll change if it means you'll shut up about it."

"Thanks, it would put my mind at ease."

The fact is, your kids absolutely hate when you nag them, so sometimes they do what you ask because they know you'll shut up once they do it. This is the situation with Ted. He probably understands Andrew's objections, but more importantly, it's seven a.m. and he doesn't want to hear any more about it. He'd much rather change the outfit.

Either way, Andrew makes some great points. For instance, he says, "I'm not saying you need to be sensitive to everyone's feelings," before Ted can object and say, "It's not my job to watch out for them." This demonstrates that Andrew is thinking two steps ahead of Ted, to cut off his objections before the really nasty remarks start flying.

Also, Andrew was probably expecting Ted to agree with him when he said, "If a shirt offended you, can you confidently say you'd walk away?" Andrew forgot to factor in that Ted doesn't want to agree with him even if he does. So, when Ted said, "Yes," Andrew made the right move by saying he'd deck someone if they offended him. Now, even if Ted comes back with, "Well, I don't think like you," Andrew can say, "I understand. But plenty of other loony birds do. So if you don't want trouble, you'll take this into account."

Clothing Doesn't Grow on Trees, Either

"I NEED THOSE JEANS, AT ANY COST."

Kate is thirteen years old and she is starting to insist on wearing only certain brands. As a middle schooler, this type of thing is really important to her. She wants to fit in, and for Kate, it feels like having the right jeans and the right clothes and the right shoes is part of being accepted. In fact, it probably is a big part of how the other girls will think of her, but most importantly, it gives Kate self-confidence to feel like she fits in when she is dressed a certain way.

Today, she is out shopping with her mother at a

store that carries all different types of clothing in a wide range of prices, and she is just dying for a certain pair of jeans.

"Oooh, Mom, what do you think of this pair?"

"They're cute. How much are they?"

"Why is that always the first question? What if they look good?"

"Why try them on, Kate, if we can't afford them? You'll only fall in love and be more upset when you can't get them."

"Uch, well, I'm trying them on."

Her mother looks at the price tag on the rack Kate got the jeans from. "That's fine. But I'm telling you now that a hundred dollars for a pair of jeans is way too much. We simply can't get them."

"Come on, Mom. *Please?* I want them soo badly."

"There are a million different pairs of jeans here, many of which I'd be perfectly happy to get for you. Look at these." She holds up another pair of jeans. "These are cute and they're a quarter of the price."

"Eeew, Marcus Jeans. Yuck, I can't wear those."

"They look exactly the same as the ones you're holding."

"Marcus Jeans are knockoffs, Mom."

"Well, excuse me. I guess you won't get anything, then. I was perfectly willing to buy these for you, but now you're being a brat. I don't have to deal with that. Come on, we have to go buy your brother sneakers."

"Uch." Kate rolls her eyes.

"Don't make a scene in the store, please, Kate."

"I'm not!" Kate says sternly as she stamps her foot, trying to stop herself from screaming out in frustration.

This situation may not sound that bad—there isn't any screaming or yelling or throwing things—but there are a lot of issues under the surface that aren't being talked about here. This is partly because Kate and her mother are out in public, but also because nobody wants to talk about the real issues.

First, there is the main issue: that Kate can't buy the jeans she wants. For the whole first part of the conversation, her mother makes that clear while she tries to ameliorate the situation (offering her another, less expensive pair of jeans), but Kate doesn't care what her mother says. She wants the jeans.

The best way to deal with this, or at least the most effective way to get through to your teen, is to talk about it when you're not in the store. You can't just say, "They're too expensive" while she's standing there holding them, because all she'll hear is "You can't have them." Also, you don't need to tell her every detail about your financial situation, you just need to be frank with her about what is too expensive for a pair of jeans.

Then, together, you can try to think of some ways to get around the prices. Maybe there is a store near you where they sell discount designer clothes. Maybe you can work out a plan for each of you to pay part of the cost. Maybe she can put it on a holiday wish list. Maybe she can buy cheaper ones and jazz them up with ribbon to make them unique, or something else she thinks is cool. Whatever it may be, discuss options together. She may not be open to this right away, as she will probably still be intent on getting the jeans, but once she realizes that's just not happening, she might open up to brainstorming, so be patient.

Even if this works, though, it's still not getting to the root of the problem, which is that she wants to fit in and thinks that expensive brand names will help. We're warning you now that even if she knows that's the real reason, she doesn't want to admit it. She probably knows that being accepted based on appearances shouldn't be important, so you can't just say something like "You know they're not real friends if they don't accept you in the clothes you have." It may have worked on *Full House*, but it's not going to work here.

Since she isn't going to admit that's why she wants the jeans (she may not even realize that's the reason), she is going to lash out at you for accusing her of it. So, don't try to have a heart-to-heart about being yourself when you're in the midst of the jeans discussion. You can have a more general talk about acceptance sometime later.

Teenage Conformity

Don't accuse your teen or her friends of being shallow or of wanting to be just like all the other kids at school. When you say, "You just want ____ because everyone else has it," your teen hears, "You're a follower. I'm disappointed in you." Because your teen knows on some level that there is some truth to your statement, she is going to become extremely defensive. So try to stay away from comments like this. It won't help the situation. She might become more insecure and defensive. She might not pay any attention at all. One thing you can count on, though, is that she won't say, "Oh, you're right! I never realized that. Thanks!"

Piercings & Tattoos

We know you hope that you will never hear the words "Can I get a tattoo?" or "Hey, what about a nipple piercing?" but it is possible that your teen is contemplating getting a tattoo or piercing—with or without your permission. Let's be honest here. Assuming it is done safely, a tattoo or piercing doesn't hurt anyone. Your first goal as a parent should be to make sure that your teen feels comfortable talking to you about the possibility of getting a tattoo or piercing. You don't want your kids to be afraid to talk to you about it, because then they will turn around and do it without consulting you. This makes it less likely that it will be done safely, and it also eliminates your opportunity to calmly and subtly talk them out of it.

Another thing you should really try to do is look at the situation through your teen's eyes. Times have changed, and it will help to remember that before you blow up at your kid. Maybe when you were in high school only thugs had tattoos, and nobody pierced anything but their ears, but today these things are pretty common.

The bottom line is that it's your teen's body, and your teen knows that, so trying to seize control will only drive a wedge between the two of you. In the end, if a teenager really wants a piercing or tattoo, he's going to get one.

You're probably thinking, "Like hell he will!" If you're still thinking like that, guess what? She might have one already, and you'll never know. Once your kid is a teenager, he or she can have piercings and tattoos you never see. We know plenty of kids who have tattoos on their hips or butt, or pierced belly buttons, and their parents have no idea. It's pretty easy.

The thing is, your teen really doesn't want to do it behind your back. She would much rather do it with your approval. Even if she doesn't want you to go with her when she gets the tattoo or piercing, if you're discussing it openly you can make sure that wherever she's going follows all the necessary safety procedures. Wouldn't you rather it happened that way?

So how do you make sure your teen feels comfortable enough to talk to you about it? Well, answer this question first: Do you comment every time you see some guy on the street with an eyebrow or lip piercing? If the answer is yes, then you need to quit it. We aren't asking you to tape your mouth shut or stop voicing your opinion, just tone it down. Instead of saying, "What an animal" when the guy walks by, say something like "Now, how does he know he wants to have holes in his body for the rest of his life?" This way your teen can start thinking about the possibility that piercings do not always close up, and that it could be a pretty permanent choice, not just an experiment.

Before It Happens: Asking Permission

"COME ON, LET ME PIERCE IT."

Lauren is fifteen years old and wants to get her belly button pierced. She knows her parents would freak out if she did it behind their backs, so she decides to ask them, and spends the week trying to think of the best way to approach them. Finally, on Saturday evening, while her parents are getting ready to go out, she comes into their bedroom.

"Hey, guys," Lauren says as she plops down on the bed.

"We'll be at the Thompsons'. The number's on

the fridge in case you need us, and Dad has his cell phone."

"Okay. So . . ."

"So . . . that 'so' sounds like you are about to ask for something."

"Dad!"

"Well, you are going to ask for something, aren't you?"

"No, you can't stay out after curfew tonight," her mother interjects.

"Jeez, you guys, I wasn't going to ask anything like that. I'm not even going out. I was just going to ask if I could get my belly button pierced. I mean, not right this second, but in the next couple of weeks. You know, before the summer."

"You must be joking," her mother says.

"No, I've really thought it over and I know it's something I want. I weighed the pros and cons and I think I'm ready. I'm fifteen and I'm going to be driving soon, and I think I'm old enough for a belly-button ring."

"I think your father and I will decide when you're old enough. And guess what? You're not."

"But, Mom! That's so unfair!"

"No discussion. A belly-button ring looks trashy, and you're too young! Lauren, I can't believe we're even having this discussion."

"I hate you guys. You're so unfair. Julie's mom said she could, Amanda already has one, and Kate has her eyebrow pierced. You're so stuck in the old days!"

"Don't speak like that to your mother, Lauren!"

"She just called me trashy—I'll say whatever I want to her!" Lauren slams the door as she rushes out of the room.

This is obviously *not* the best way for the conversation to play out. When your teen comes to ask for permission before doing something like getting a piercing, you should be happy that she is even asking. You really need to take advantage of the opportunity to make an impression on her before she does something you don't approve of. By asking you, she's put the ball in your court, and you then have the power to at least delay things for a while. Plus, the conversation just doesn't have to turn out like this.

It's not that you can't be firm and tell your teen she absolutely cannot get her belly button pierced; for a lot of teens, that will come across quite clearly and they won't want to disobey you. Once you see that she's not giving up easily, though, you'll have to change your approach. So, for example, in the situation above, it's okay for the mother to say, "Your father and I will decide when you're old enough." Even if your teen says, "That's so unfair," it doesn't mean she doesn't hear you. She just wants it so badly that it's natural for her to be unhappy when she can't get it. What's more important for you to focus on is why she's getting so upset at you.

The main reason that Lauren gets so angry, to the point that she would say she hates her parents, is *not* because she can't get a belly-button ring. She pretty much knew the answer she'd get going into the conversation. She's angry because she is offended by the way her mother treated her. Lauren would be able to accept "No, you're too young," but when her mother says, "That's so trashy," she hears, "Eew, what bad taste you have. I can't believe you would want something like that. I think it's ugly, and your opinion isn't valid." Lauren obviously doesn't share her mother's feelings, so insulting the piercing in general is going to piss her off much more than just being told no.

"LET'S MAKE A DEAL."

"Hey, guys," Lauren says as she plops down on the bed.

"We'll be at the Thompsons'. The number's on the fridge in case you need us, and Dad has his cell phone."

"Okay. So . . ."

"So . . . that 'so' sounds like you are about to ask for something."

"Dad!"

"Well, you are going to ask for something, aren't you?"

"No, you can't stay out after curfew tonight," her mother interjects.

"Jeez, you guys, I wasn't going to ask anything like that. I'm not even going out. I was just going to ask if I could get my belly button pierced. I mean, not right this second, but in the next couple of weeks. You know, before the summer."

"You must be joking," her mother says.

"No, I've really thought it over and I know it's something I want. I weighed the pros and cons and I think I'm ready."

"Come on, Lauren, don't you think you're still kind of young?" her father asks.

"No, not really, Dad. Things are different nowadays. I mean, I'm fifteen and I'm going to be driving soon. I think I'm old enough for a belly-button ring."

"We know that, Lauren. I think we would just feel more comfortable if you waited. You understand that, don't you?"

"I knew you'd say something like that! But it's my belly button, not yours!"

I HATE YOU!

That phrase could be a chapter, or even a book, of its own—it's important to realize what teens really mean when they say it.

It doesn't always literally mean that we hate you. In fact, most of the time we're only saying it out of frustration, in the heat of the argument. Most teens wouldn't say "I hate you" when they are actually thinking rationally (i.e., while they are not fighting with you), because they don't really mean it.

When we're fighting with you and we say it, it's usually just for lack of a better and more descriptive phrase. When we're mad, we're not feeling very articulate, and we don't want to spend the time to think of a sentence that will really tell you how we feel. "I hate you" is just *much* easier to get out, and seems to group all the emotions we're feeling into one single, powerful, all-purpose phrase that we can hurl at you.

So, like in Lauren's situation, parents need to take "I hate you" in stride. We're not saying you can't reprimand your teen for saying it, or being rude to you; we're just saying that we know it's not *nice* to say "I hate you," and we don't really mean it, anyway, but in the heat of the moment it can slip out.

"Yeah, but as long as you're not legal, we get to decide what happens to that belly button," her father says, then sticks out his tongue at her.

"Fine, I won't do it this year, but what about next school year?"

"How about we see when the time comes?"

"I can't win in this house!" Lauren throws her arms up in the air.

"Nope. You can't." Her father flashes her a big smile.

"But, seriously, Lauren, you have to understand that this is the first time we've heard about it, so you're taking us by surprise. Why don't you give us some time to think about it, and you take the next few months too. You need to make sure you *really* want this. Even though I know you've thought about it, as your mother I feel the need to emphasize you are making a hole in your body."

"I know. I know. Just think about it."

"Okay, sweetie."

Even though Lauren didn't get what she wanted in this situation, she sees it as a success. It's successful in her eyes because she didn't fight with her parents about it, so she feels she came off as somewhat mature; she also sort of "warned" her parents that she wants this and now they know she won't give it up. It's also a success for the parents, because they've satisfied Lauren for the time being instead of saying, "No! Never! You can't!" and they were calm and kept the tone of the conversation lighthearted.

They may very well have this conversation again, since they decided to put it off until Lauren is older, but this was a good decision because it saved them all from fighting at that moment, and possibly from more fights that would have resulted every time Lauren approached them. (Just remember, a teen can think she is older after two weeks, so don't be surprised if she comes back to you in two weeks and says, "Can I have it now?")

The tactics the parents used to keep this situation positive and upbeat were to talk to Lauren about the piercing rather than saying, "Absolutely not, no discussion." No teen is going to accept or be happy with that. Even if we don't get our way, we want the opportunity to plead our case.

In this situation, Lauren was happy to be able to answer questions like "Don't you think you're still kind of young?" The parents made it a dialogue; it wasn't just them yelling at Lauren. Almost more crucial, they didn't lecture her or over-react, like she had asked them for a bag of marijuana. Asking to get a piercing is *not* the end of the world, so treating it like it is a big deal will only bore your teen (as she has to listen to you question her about *why* she really wants the ring, or hear about how it could get infected) or make her angry (like in the first scenario).

Piercing Without Permission: How to Deal

If your teen comes home with a new piercing that she didn't ask you about, you have two basic choices: you can make her take it out or you can let her keep it. We can't tell you whether or not to make your kid take out the piercing, that's up to you, but we can tell you the best way to make them take it out. (If you're letting her keep it, that's kind of a no-brainer: you tell her she can keep it.)

"YOU MUST BE KIDDING. TAKE THAT OUT RIGHT NOW!"

Lauren has gotten her belly button pierced without asking. Now she is on vacation with her family at the beach, and it's no longer possible for her to hide the piercing. She decides it's best to bring it to her parents' attention before they notice on their own.

"So, Mom, Dad, I have a little something to show you." Lauren's parents both turn to look at her. She lifts her shirt to expose her two-week-old belly-button ring.

"Surprise."

"Oh my God!" her mother shrieks.

"Take it out right now—"

"But, Dad!"

"No! Take it out. Go to the bathroom and take it out. You were *never* given permission to do that, so go take it out right now."

"No. It's my stomach. I'll decide what to do with it, and I'm *not* taking it out."

"Please, Lauren," her mother pleads.

"I shouldn't even have shown it to you! Uch, I'm not taking it out!" Lauren storms off.

"Get back here, Lauren!" her father shouts after her.

This is basically the worst possible outcome; not only won't she take out the belly-button ring, but she also gets angry and storms off. Her parents have set up the situation so it will be even harder for them to ever get her to take it out. The first thing they could have done to avoid this was stay calm and not make any demands. Instead of exploding, they should have tried their best to make it a discussion.

A parent's best bet here is not to beg (like Lauren's mother) and not to command (like Lauren's father), but rather to acknowledge their anger ("Lauren, we can't believe you went and did this without asking") and then try to speak about it rationally ("Okay, Lauren, let's just be rational here. Obviously, we want you to take it out, so let us explain why").

When Lauren's father says, "You were *never* given permission to do that," Lauren just hears, "We're the bosses of you and you have to take it out. We don't have a real reason except that we don't want you to have what you want." You have to explain *why* you're so unhappy about it.

Is it because she didn't ask? Because she's too young? Because she might have gotten an infection? Because you think it looks bad? Well, whatever the reason is, you'll have to try to explain your reasons the best you can without making accusations ("Now you look trashy" or "Only sluts get belly-button rings").

Also, remember that there's a difference between *explaining* and *lecturing*. With a lecture, your teen will be in another

Before and After "no"

Although to a parent the difference between doing something without asking and doing it after being told "no" may seem minimal, to a teen it is not. To teens, doing something without asking can often look like a better option than taking the chance of being told no. It seems better to just do it and hope it goes over well with your parents (even if you really know it won't) than to ask and then have to disobey them to get what you want.

So when you're about to yell at your kid because she got something pierced, try to put yourself in her shoes. "Does she think she's disobeying me or just taking a chance?" Yes, she knows you'll be mad either way, but in her mind she hasn't disobeyed you, so she doesn't think she deserves to be treated as if she did.

world before you've said five words and won't hear anything else you say. So, you need to make it interactive; you get to explain, but so does your teen. You want to make your teen feel like she is going to be heard, otherwise she'll just storm out of the room.

Piercing reality note: Just remember, asking your kid to take out her piercing isn't really punishment for her if she's already had it for more than a few weeks. The hole won't close up, so it won't be a problem for her to take it out around you, and then put it back in a week later when she's with her friends and out of your sight.

"LET'S MAKE A DEAL.": VERSION TWO

Lauren shows her parents her new belly-button ring.

"Oh my God!" her mother shrieks.

"Take it out right now—"

"But, Dad!"

"Sorry, it's just that . . . well, that you never even asked us about this. I mean, what do you expect me to say?"

"I know, I know. But you don't have to freak out."

"You're right. But I still want you to take it out."

"I *knew* you'd say that! That's why I didn't show it to you."

"Look, Lauren, we're just kind of shocked. I mean your father and I had no idea you had that, then you lift your shirt and there's a hole in your stomach."

"Okay, Mom, I get the point. But why do I have to take it out?"

"Well, I could go on about that for a while, but basically because you didn't ask—"

"And because you're too young and you could have gotten hurt and—" Lauren's father adds.

"Yeah, well, I knew you'd say no if I asked."

"So why did you do it then, if you knew we wouldn't approve?" her mother asks.

"I don't know, I just wanted it so badly."

"We understand the feeling, but that doesn't mean you're going to get away with it."

"Yeah, I know, I know."

"Look, Lauren, maybe in a couple of months or next year we can talk about this again. You know, if you still really want it as badly after thinking about it that long, maybe you will be ready to get one. You understand that, don't you?"

"Yeah, I guess. Can I just keep it for the rest of vacation, though?"

"Nice try."

This went well because both Lauren and her parents got to voice their opinions and their reasoning, and because they were able to express their real emotions (surprised, angry, frustrated, etc.), but then calm down and actually talk about *why* Lauren was going to take it out. When her parents were honest about their surprise, Lauren could also be honest ("I knew you'd say no if I asked").

Lauren's parents didn't just lecture her about why she had to take it out; there was a real sense of back-and-forth. Also, just like if she had asked permission first, it can't hurt to tell her that if she still wants it once she's older, you can all discuss it again. You don't have to make any promises, but knowing that it's not a closed issue will give your teen some satisfaction.

The Harsh Realities of Teenage Tattoos

Whether you like it or not, many teens have fake IDs, and the ones who don't can get them if they really want to, which means your teen doesn't need you to come with him in order to get a tattoo. We know this sounds pretty harsh, but it's the truth. If your teen wants a tattoo *that* badly, he will get around you.

We are here to help you figure out a system so that your teen will *want* to talk to you about a tattoo before getting one, because, frankly, the last thing you want is your teen going to some unsanitary hole-in-the-wall on his own because he didn't feel comfortable enough to approach you about it. Unfortunately, you as the parent will need to decide if you are willing to sacrifice your standards on the tattoo issue in order to keep your teen safe. This doesn't mean that you need to act as if you approve; you just have to be willing to not stand in his way. If you are, read on.

Like piercing, the first thing you want to do is start dropping comments about how bad tattoos are. You don't want to say things like "tattoos are so unattractive," though, because your teen will just disagree. You want to say things like "It sucks for that guy. Nobody's going to hire him if he wants to get a job. Did you know that businesses think it ruins their image when they have workers with tattoos?" Or, you could say something like "That guy is going to hate his tattoo when he's older. When he begins to age the tattoo will lose its shape and it will become all ugly and distorted. People really ought to think this stuff through more thoroughly." These comments are really important. Although you are not directing them at your teen, it gets him thinking about the long-term and practical aspects of tattoos.

Also, you could approach the tattoo situation the same way we demonstrated in the piercing scenario: make a deal and try to hold him off for a while. If your teen reacts really poorly to that approach and announces that he's going out to get a tattoo on his own, you can still do one of these things:

- Explain that tattoos need to be approached in a safe manner. Getting it done at any random place is extremely dangerous.
- Propose he try henna before he makes a very, very permanent decision. Henna is a dye that isn't permanent, but lasts about a month. Tell him that you want him to get the same tattoo he's planning to, but drawn in henna first. If he is still absolutely and completely positive he wants the tattoo after a few months of henna, you will reconsider your position. This buys you some time.

Chapter 6

"Money *Doesn't* Grow on Trees?":

Teen Finance

We know you want to give your kids whatever they want, because they're your kids, and making them happy is the best thing in the world, but if you did that, you'd end up with kids who expect to just get whatever they want. Ideally, by the time your child is a teenager, you have taught him the value of money and you've established a way for him to acquire money without taking everything for granted. Whether they have to work around the house to receive allowance, they get a job to earn a paycheck, or you hand it out every time they ask for it, a system that works for your teens should be established.

Teens like to think they are independent but we all know that without our parents' help, we would be unable to do the things we do. It's hard for teenagers to think about the value of money when a movie or bowling or a new shirt is tempting them; therefore we rely on our parents to prevent us from exercising bad judgment (or from taking advantage of you).

While teens feel the need for financial independence, they also rely on their parents to teach them how to value and manage money. Any financial arrangement between teens and parents should help the teen feel independent but should also ensure that the parents still maintain control.

When parents hand their teen two credit cards and an unlimited budget, chances are the teen is thinking, "Wow, money does grow on trees!" The teen thinks that whenever he wants money he can get it. If he comes to his parents looking for money and is asked, "What happened to the money I gave you last night?" the teen won't understand why he needs to explain where the money went when there's always more money available. No teen should live in a fantasy bubble like that, and no teen wants to be friends with someone who does.

PLAYING POOL: AN EXPENSIVE LUXURY

Billy and his friends like to go out to play pool on Saturday nights. It has become an expensive habit. Henry, Billy's father, wants him to have fun, but he thinks it's probably time for Billy to start taking on more responsibility by paying for some of his own luxuries, like pool. Henry decides he'll pay for a portion of the games and ask Billy to earn the money to pay for the rest. If Billy can't get a job, Henry will offer to pay him to do different chores around the house that he wouldn't normally do.

"So, Billy, I was talking to your mother and I know how much you enjoy playing pool with the guys, but it's a lot of money. Twenty bucks doesn't sound like that much, but when you play every Saturday night for fifty-two weeks it becomes a different story."

"I didn't really think about it."

"Okay. Now I'm asking you to start thinking about it. Mom and I want you to start paying for pool. I mean, money doesn't grow on trees, so you need to learn to appreciate it."

"Who said I didn't appreciate it?" snaps Billy.

"Well, playing pool every single weekend is sort of ridiculous, Billy."

"That's your opinion and that's not my problem."

"Well, it's also my money."

"Whatever. So, now when all my friends go and play, I'm supposed to just stay home by myself? I can't ask them all to stop playing just because *you* think it's too expensive."

"That's not what I said. I want you to get a job and start paying for some of it yourself. Mom and I don't mind picking it up twice a month, but after that, you need to help out."

"Yeah, how do you expect me to do that? Who's gonna hire me? You can't expect me to get a job just like that!" Billy snaps his fingers.

"Maybe not, but I will if you can't find a job in the next month. Start doing some extra chores around the house, and we'll figure something out. Let's start tomorrow with some work around the house, and over the weekend we'll start looking for a job."

Billy rolls his eyes as he walks away.

Since this is a new proposition, you will want to give your teenager a few weeks' warning, and an explanation for your decision. If you don't, your teenager will end up feeling as if you had said, "You aren't entitled to have fun. Grow up. You're not a kid anymore. This isn't your money. You didn't work for it, I did."

The first thing Henry should have done is say something like "I know I'm probably catching you off guard, but this is something we want you to start thinking about. We won't start doing this for another few weeks, so it's nothing to get stressed about." The second your teen hears about something involving money and responsibility, he's going to start bugging out, so it's a good move to start off by saying, "This is nothing to worry about. We'll figure it all out together," to put your kid's mind at ease.

Henry took a wrong turn when he said, "Playing pool every single weekend is sort of ridiculous." Your kid's already doing it, so putting him down for something he obviously values, even if it's only entertainment, is pointless. It will only insult your kid and make him angry.

If you feel the need to make the point that playing pool so often is a little excessive, then you can say something like "Okay, here's your weekly entertainment budget. It's enough to play pool every other week, and still do some other things, or you can play pool every week and sacrifice movies and CDs." Now your *kid* has to decide to cut back, get a job, or sacrifice something else in order to play pool every week; now he has to make choices about money. Which is to say, he has to learn that it doesn't grow on trees.

Also, it's important that your kid understands that your money isn't always his money, and that he needs to ask permission to use it. Still, you shouldn't make him feel like he owes you a favor every time you pay for something like a game of pool. If he does, he'll never be completely comfortable around you, and he'll probably resent you for it.

Once you've made the decision to buy your teenager something, you shouldn't use it later to manipulate him, like "I paid for your movie last night, so help me wash the car today." It's totally okay to ask him to help you with the car, but if you do it like that, he won't react well. He will hear, "I only give you things so I can make you do what I want." In the same way, when Henry says, "It's my money," Billy hears, "You'll do what I say because I pay the bills, not because it's the right thing for you to do. Don't ever forget I'm boss." Yes, you are the boss, but flaunting it makes you come off like a real jerk, and you won't make any progress with your kid. He won't understand that this is about learning to appreciate the value of a dollar; he will think it's about you and your need for an ego trip.

A MORE POSITIVE OUTCOME: PLAYING POOL

"So, Billy, I was talking to your mother and I know how much you enjoy playing pool with the guys, but it's starting to become expensive. Twenty bucks doesn't sound so bad, but when you play every Saturday night for fifty-two weeks it becomes a different story."

"I didn't really think about it."

"Okay, well, I've been thinking about it a bunch, and I'd like you to start paying for some of the games of pool on the weekends. I know this seems really out of the blue but you are seventeen now, so I think it's time. Of course, we wouldn't ask you to do this immediately, but it's something we want you to start thinking about."

"How exactly do you expect me to come up with the money to pay for this?" snaps Billy. "Like you said, I'm seventeen. No one is going to hire me. So if I can't come up with the money, you're just going to stop me from playing pool with my friends?"

"That is not what I'm saying at all. We want you to have fun with your friends, but pool every weekend is getting expensive. I'm not asking you to stop completely, but you are old enough to start paying for some of your own luxuries. I'll pay for three out of the four Saturdays a month for the next few months, and until you can find a job you can start doing extra chores in the house that we'll pay you for to cover the other weekend, but after the first few months I think we should talk about your responsibilities and look at the situation again."

"Fine. Whatever."

Don't take it personally if your teen is snotty with you. Your teen is going to have an attitude no matter how well you handle the conversation. After all, you are telling him that it's time he starts learning to make and manage his own money; that's new to your teen, and it's certainly not a fun and exciting adventure he's eager to embark on.

Henry makes a number of good moves, starting with the way he opens the conversation. By saying, "I know you and your friends really enjoy playing pool," it's obvious to Billy that Henry's not setting out to ruin his fun. It's also great that Henry says, "Twenty bucks doesn't sound so bad, but when you play every Saturday night for fifty-two weeks it becomes a different story." Teens often forget to put their spending in perspective and to think of all the things they spend money on in the course of a day. They forget that all those one-dollar bills eventually add up to a significant amount of money.

Henry didn't go into this conversation assuming that Billy didn't know how expensive pool is, which was a good thing; this way Billy can't accuse Henry of thinking that. Also, Henry was smart to recognize that this conversation was probably a lot of information to throw at a teenager so quickly, so it was great that he told Billy that there is no rush and that they would slowly ease into this new system.

Is My Teen Ready for a Credit Card?

At some point or another, you have probably thought about giving your teen a credit card. If your teen is now sixteen or seventeen, you probably feel a credit card is a great thing for her to have in case of an emergency with the car, like if she gets a flat tire or runs out of cash to pay for gas. While this sounds like a great idea at the beginning, you may want to check with your teen first.

This may come as a shock to you, but not every teen wants the responsibility that accompanies a credit card. An average teenager probably loses a wallet at least once a year throughout high school. This being the case, you wouldn't want a credit card in that wallet, and neither would your teen. Of course your teen probably hasn't thought about all this, but once you point out that with a credit card comes more responsibility, she may not want one after all. If you or your teenager is uncomfortable with the idea, consider trying a debit card, or designated "emergency money," first. (See below for information about that option.)

"DO FASHION EMERGENCIES COUNT?"

Brandon and Kelly decide that it's time to talk to their seventeen-year-old daughter, Brenda, about getting her a credit card.

"Brenda, we've given it a lot of thought, and because you are driving now, Dad and I think it's time you had a credit card of your own for emergency purposes. What do you think?"

"Sounds good to me. Order away."

"Well, don't just shrug it off like it's no big deal. A credit card is a really big responsibility. You won't be

allowed to use this for shopping or whatever it is
you waste money on these days. This card is just for
emergencies."

"What if it's a fashion emergency?" says Brenda, sarcastically.

"This isn't a joke, Brenda."

"You guys shouldn't be so uptight about it. It's just
a piece of plastic," says Brenda, rolling her eyes and
giggling.

Even though it looks like Kelly approached the situation
really well with Brenda, she didn't. She starts off well by saying that they have given the credit card idea a lot of thought,
and pointing out the purpose of the card. It's after the first
line leaves her mouth that the conversation goes downhill.

When Kelly says, "Well, don't just shrug it off like it's no
big deal. . . . You won't be allowed to use this for shopping or
whatever it is you waste money on these days," Brenda is going to become not only defensive but extremely insulted.
Whether or not Brenda really wastes a lot of money and time
on shopping, it isn't something that should be discussed in
the context of ordering a credit card.

If Kelly wants to have a productive conversation about
the responsibilities of having a credit card, then she shouldn't
use words like *waste*. She should say something more like
"Before we make this decision, we need to sit down and discuss the rules for this credit card and when you can and can't
use it." This can be her rational, nonprovocative segue into a
conversation on credit card rules. No one gets hurt, and all
the issues can be addressed.

I CAN'T CONTROL MYSELF.
DON'T GIVE ME THE CREDIT CARD!

"Brenda, we've given it a lot of thought, and because you are driving now, Dad and I think it's time you had a credit card of your own for emergency purposes. What do you think?"

"Sounds good to me. Order away."

"Well, don't just shrug it off like it's no big deal. A credit card is a really big responsibility."

"I know that. I understand what a credit card is."

"All we are saying is that if you were to lose the credit card, it would be really bad for all of us, because someone could just pick it up and start using it like it was their own. Someone could easily charge thousands of dollars before we even knew the card was missing. It's all really scary, but if you think you are responsible enough to have one; then we are willing to trust your instincts. We just think this is something you really ought to consider, first. A lot of teens don't think they're ready, because they have a tendency to lose things, and because things can easily get stolen at school. If you feel like that stuff isn't an issue for you, then we will order you the card."

"Well, what's the alternative? Without the credit card I don't have a way out if I'm in trouble with the car."

"There are other ways we could work it out. We could give you 'emergency money,' or we could hide it someplace in the car, or in your wallet, or we could get you a debit card."

"Oh, I'd much rather do that. Less pressure."

or **her response could be**

"Oh, well, let's try the credit card. If I get uncomfortable having it, we can always cancel it."

You have to trust your teen's instincts. If she thinks she is ready for a credit card after you have clearly laid out the reasons you have doubt and the responsibilities that accompany a credit card, then you should try it out. Start slowly if you are really worried that your teen might lose the credit card— if the reason she has it is for when she drives, leave the credit card in a special place that you both know is safe. When she does drive, she can take the credit card with her, and when she's done she can return the card to the same spot instead of carrying it around all day and night when it's unnecessary for her to do so.

It was important in this conversation for Kelly to discuss the reasons why a stolen credit card is such a bad thing. If she hadn't, then the conversation would probably end with Brenda thinking, "My mom overreacts about everything. It's just a credit card." Your teen needs to understand where your anxiety comes from, and Kelly used one good way to approach a teen on the issue.

Also, it was smart of Kelly to mention that other teens were worried about credit card responsibilities, and that some don't get them because of their worries. Often, in matters of increasing responsibility, teens feel like they are being challenged. If Kelly had left that out of the conversation, Brenda might have said, "Yeah, I want the credit card," because she didn't want to look like a wimp.

It may sound crazy, but your teen's decision is influenced by whether the in crowd is saying yes or no. By presenting alternatives to getting a credit card, Kelly makes it easier for Brenda to reach a rational decision.

"I KNOW MOM WILL KILL ME, BUT I HAVE TO HAVE THIS SKIRT!"

One afternoon, Kimmy, a fifteen-year-old with her own credit card and an eye for fashion, is out shopping with some friends. She spots a skirt and "falls in love" with it. She decides to try it on even though she knows

Paying Teens to Do Chores

There's really no right or wrong approach to this issue; it is completely based on your own beliefs and your specific circumstances. The one thing that we can say is that teenagers understand when their parents tell them that they have to make their beds, clean the dishes, or do laundry. Yes, we might groan each time you remind us to do one of these chores, and we might put it off for as long as possible, but we understand that doing them is just part of life, and no teenager really thinks they have to be paid for it. That's not to say that paying your teen (especially when he's younger) isn't a decent incentive to get him to do these basic chores; depending on your situation, it could also be helpful in teaching your teen the value of money and how to manage it. So getting paid to do chores isn't something teens think they deserve (which is not to say they aren't concerned about getting money *somehow*), so it shouldn't be something you are worrying about.

she can't buy it. After trying it on, she's absolutely dying for the skirt. She weighs the pros and cons in her head: she only has two skirts for spring and this one can be fancy or casual, but on the other hand she knows her mother would find eighty dollars way too expensive for a skirt, and she doesn't really *need* it. Within a matter of minutes, her conscience has lost the battle and she hands over her credit card.

Later that night, Kimmy decides to show her mother the skirt.

"Another skirt, Kimmy? How much was it?" She turns over the tag hanging off the skirt. "Eighty dollars? Have you gone nuts?"

"No, see, I only have two other skirts, and this one is so versatile, Mom—"

"Let me tell you right now, Kimmy, there's no way you can justify this one. I don't care if this skirt was five dollars, you know you're not to use the credit card to buy stuff for yourself without my permission. I mean, Kimmy, how could you think I wouldn't mind?"

"But I love it, Mom, and I swear I don't want any more spring clothing . . . or wait, this could be one of my birthday presents, an early one, you know?"

"Just *stop*. Look, this is ridiculous. Stop making excuses and trying to explain yourself. You're just throwing money out the window like it's nothing. I work hard and it's not so that you can go throwing money around."

"That's so *not* true. You're so out of it. I thought about it before I bought the skirt, okay? I know you work hard. Jeez. You can't accuse me of something like that."

"Well, you're not exactly acting like you appreciate me or know the value of money, so tomorrow morning you can go return that skirt. I *hope* you kept the receipt. Oh, and you can forget about going out shopping with your friends anymore. In fact, I think we better adjust your allowance so there's no money for extra spending."

"Are you crazy? What do you mean?"

"Me? Crazy? I'm not the one who messed up. What I meant about your allowance is that I'm only going to factor in money for the bus, lunch at school, and an emergency twenty dollars that you *better* not touch unless it's a life-or-death situation."

"This is insane! I made barely *one* mistake and now you're treating me like a five-year-old! Arrgggh, I can't stand living in this house."

"You made the mess yourself this time. There's nobody else to blame for this one, so learn to live with it."

Basically, Kimmy's mother has the right to be angry here, because her daughter didn't ask to buy the skirt and used bad judgment. That still doesn't mean that yelling at Kimmy will solve the problem, though. Okay, maybe Kimmy will learn her lesson and won't buy something without asking again, but this situation definitely didn't go well. It could have been an opportunity for Kimmy and her mother to *talk* and for her to reinforce the rules for the credit card.

Kimmy gets angry mainly because she knows she messed up and she can't bear to hear her mother telling her over and over again how much she messed up. Kimmy's conscience is probably giving her a hard time, so she already feels guilty; when her mother keeps making the same point, making her feel worse and worse, she finally turns it around and gets mad at her mother.

When her mother says to "Stop making excuses" and that

"There's nobody to blame for this one," Kimmy is hearing, "You messed up big time and now you're going to pay big time and I'm not going to let you live it down." Also, when her mother accuses her of not knowing the value of money or appreciating her mother's hard work, Kimmy is offended and becomes defensive.

So, like we've said before, it's really important to avoid accusatory language or tone, because there's no way that will make your kid want to communicate with you. It will just make them shut you out.

Even though Kimmy probably feels bad enough, we're not saying she should get off the hook, but for this to play out in a better way, Kimmy's mother could have talked to her about it calmly, rather than freaking out. Nobody got hurt, there was no serious danger, and there's a good chance you can get your money back (but if not, there are still ways to deal with it—listed below). All you need to do now is make sure it doesn't happen again. There's really no reason for you to get extremely upset or start yelling unless this wasn't the first time.

"YOU BUY WITHOUT ASKING, I SIT YOU DOWN TO TALK ABOUT IT."

Kimmy has just told her mother about the skirt she bought without permission.

"Okay, Kimmy, what exactly were you thinking when you bought that? You know I'd never let you get that."

"But, Mom, it's so cute—"

"That has nothing to do with it."

"*Please*, Mom . . ."

"Kimmy, you know you're returning it, so there's no reason to test me. I just don't understand why you bought it without asking. It makes me feel like I haven't taught you anything about the value of a dollar. You understand why I say that, right?"

"No, I mean, you have. It's not that I thought it was acceptable, really, it was just that I couldn't exactly help myself . . . if that makes sense. I don't know, I made a mistake, I guess. If I had a bigger allowance then I wouldn't have to ask, but I don't."

"I understand. I just think you need to think more before you act impulsively, you know? Just because you don't have enough money of your own, you can't buy something without asking."

"Yeah, that makes sense. I hope you know I don't do things like this a lot. It was just a one-time thing, and yes, I know I still have to return it, but I just want you to know that."

"To know that you won't do it again?"

"Yeah, and know that I know why you're mad."

"Okay, that's a good thing. Maybe you'll take a break from shopping with your friends for a little, maybe check out a museum or something?"

"Right, Mom."

This conversation went well because Kimmy's mother made it easy for Kimmy to say what she was actually thinking, without feeling like it would get her in trouble. For example, when her mother says, "You understand why I say that, right?" Kimmy doesn't feel like her mother is yelling at her for using bad judgment, but rather that she wants to find out why Kimmy bought the skirt and to be sure she can trust her daughter in the future. In fact, Kimmy sees this as an opportunity to explain what she was thinking; maybe try to make a case for herself and make sure her mother knows that she under-stands she did something wrong, so she doesn't lose her trust.

Probably the most important part of all is that Kimmy felt comfortable admitting she had made a mistake. We've said over and over again that teenagers hate to admit it when they're wrong, and that's true, but sometimes admitting it is the only way to get through a conversation with a parent. Teenagers don't feel so bad about it if they think nobody's going to use it against them, or say "I told you so!"

No teen *ever* wants to set up an "I told you so" for her parents. In fact, that's one of the best ways to make sure your teen won't talk to you: act holier than thou, or like you knew what was going to happen all along, while your teen is *just now* figuring it out.

If she didn't keep the receipt or there is no way of return-ing the item, there are ways for her to make the money back—she may not do it happily or willingly but she will do it because she knows she messed up and it's her responsibility.

By the way, if you were thinking that this issue seems like something that you will only have to worry about with girls, you're mistaken. There are many boys who will apply the same "logic" Kimmy did when out shopping for sports equip-ment, video games, even certain clothing or accessories. This situation can come up any time a teenager *really* wants some-thing and loses a battle with his conscience over it.

If your teen has done "irreversible" damage (i.e., bought something that cannot be returned), you obviously can't just let her keep the item, or else she'll never learn. Once you've made sure she understands the issues discussed above, you could consider some of these ideas to deal with the situation:

- Take it away and make her work for it; make her do odd jobs around the house, and give it back to her once she has earned it. This could be a good time to introduce to your teen the idea of getting a job and working to have her own money. This way, when she's worried you won't approve a purchase like a skirt she likes, she can buy it with money that she has worked for.

- Donate it to charity.
- Save it until the next occasion when she would receive a present and make that the present instead.

"But You Never Said Don't Buy Beer"

When you give your teenager money to go out on a Saturday night, you expect that he will spend that money responsibly and not on beer. Unfortunately, if you don't specify exactly what they can and can't spend the money on, teens won't think they're in the wrong when they choose to spend the money on beer or cigarettes. Although they know it's sleazy, teens are very good at interpreting their parents in a completely literal way when it suits their purposes.

You have to ask your teen what he is doing and what he thinks he will spend the money on *before* he goes out. Then, follow up the next morning. Ask him how he spent the money, and ask for the change. If you set up a system so that your teen knows you are carefully monitoring how he spends his money, he is less likely to take a risk and buy something inappropriate.

Emergency Money

It's pretty common for parents to want their kids to have an emergency ten or twenty with them all the time. This is money teens should only touch if their wallet is stolen or if they're in a life-or-death situation—not when they don't have enough to buy a new CD they really want. In theory this is a great idea; the problem is that teens often spend that emergency money on things that aren't what their parents would classify as emergencies.

So, first things first: you have to lay down the law of the household and define what the money can be spent on. The best thing to do is talk to them beforehand, when you first give them the emergency money, about what it is and when it is supposed to be used, *as well as* what will happen if it is misused and why.

Make sure your teen knows you won't overlook abusing emergency money. It's highly possible that it may happen once or twice, but your teen should want to fight off the temptation rather than give in easily because he thinks there won't be any consequences.

If your teen already carries emergency money but you haven't had a conversation about rules and consequences yet, you might want to take a minute to explain why he has the money and why you would be upset if he used it. Include both safety reasons and reasons concerning the value of money. It's never too late to briefly explain something (hint: don't lecture, just mention).

"IT WAS AN EMERGENCY! THE BASKETBALL SHOES ARE ONLY ON SALE UNTIL TONIGHT."

Jacob is fifteen years old and loves basketball. One afternoon, he is on his way home from a pickup game with a couple friends when he sees a pair of basketball sneakers he's been dying for in the window of a shoe store. They're on sale, but he's ten dollars short—unless he dips into the backup money his parents make him carry at all times. He decides to spend the ten dollars—half the backup money—reasoning that he'll pay his dad back later, and it's only ten bucks, after all.

The following weekend, Jacob is about to leave for the night to meet a couple friends.

"Okay, Dad, I'll be home around eleven. See you later," Jacob says as he pops his head into the kitchen where his father is eating dinner.

"That's fine. You have your cell phone and wallet and your—"

"Yes, Dad, I have everything."

"—and your backup twenty separate from the rest of your money, just in case?"

"Oh yeah, I forgot to ask you—can I get another ten bucks for backup?"

"Where did the other ten go? You didn't have an emergency, did you?"

"Oh, I'll pay you back when I get my birthday money from Grandma next week, but I spent ten on the new Nikes."

"You mean you spent half the money I gave you to carry for an *emergency*? Does that mean *nothing* to you? Or did you not even listen when I explained you're not to touch that money unless your wallet is stolen or something like that?"

"Jeez, I heard you, Dad. I didn't think it was such a big deal."

"Well, it *is* a big deal. That's what emergencies are: big deals. Don't you get that you're actually supposed to do what I tell you? You weren't supposed to *touch* that money and you did. I guess you have no respect for the safety guidelines I set or the rules about money we agreed to. How could you possibly rationalize something like that? 'It's the new Nikes, that's *obviously* an emergency!' It's like you don't think!"

"You're going nuts for *no* reason! You don't even let me speak, you just yell and yell. Maybe that's why I don't listen, because you're always getting upset when I didn't do anything wrong! I don't have to take this!" Jacob storms out of the kitchen and out the front door to meet his friends.

Of course Jacob's father has a reason to be upset. He is probably thinking about what could have happened if Jacob had been in an emergency with no money, and he hates to think his son is disregarding everything he says, but the way he handles the situation certainly won't make it any better.

The main reason the conversation went in the wrong direction was that Jacob felt like he was only being screamed at and accused of not listening ("I guess you have no respect for . . ."). Also, being mocked by his father ("It's the new Nikes, that's *obviously* an emergency!") didn't help.

At the beginning of the conversation, Jacob wants to explain to his father why he spent the ten dollars, but his father makes that impossible by turning the discussion into a screaming match. When parents say things like "What is the matter with you?" or "It's like you don't think," it's basically like inviting a teen not to respond; it's almost guaranteed to leave him completely offended and furious, and in no mood to answer your questions.

It doesn't matter that Jacob may have known he shouldn't spend the money on the shoes, because when his father says "You don't think," he hears, "You're dumb and immature and don't understand the consequences of things, and you should just give up trying to defend yourself, because you can't." Right then and there, Jacob is going to throw in the towel.

Jacob may still scream at his father, drop a couple insults in here and there, but he no longer believes that he and his father can have a civil conversation about the money. Jacob can't explain his rationale (even if he knows what he did was wrong, he will have *some* explanation) and his father can't explain why this kind of thing infuriates him so much.

LET ME EXPLAIN THE REASON WHY I'M ANGRY YOU USED THE TWENTY

"Wait. So you used *half* your *emergency* money on basketball shoes?"

"Yeah, but I'm going to pay you back—"

"But that's not the point, Jacob. Your birthday is next week, and you could have asked for the shoes. I'm just upset because of the principle, you know?"

"Yeah, I guess. . . ."

"Look, I understand that it can be tempting to have easy access to twenty bucks, but there's a reason that you're not supposed to spend it. It's partly safety, but it also concerns me that you just spent it freely without thinking about it."

"You mean without thinking about the consequences?"

"Yeah, and you don't seem to have really thought about the cost, and just went ahead and spent the money like it was Monopoly money. I mean, is that fair to say?"

"Well, not really, to tell you the truth. I thought about it, and I knew I was going into the emergency money. It wasn't that I thought I could throw money around at all. I just knew I could pay you back soon and I didn't think it was so bad to use some of the money. I mean, it's not like I was walking around without a dime."

"That's true, but in an emergency ten dollars might very well not have been enough. Do you understand why I am upset that you made the decision to go into the emergency money?"

"Yeah, I understand that, but I want you to know it's not like I just act without thinking about things at all."

"I understand."

A conversation like this is so positive because there is so much give-and-take; teen and parent are both making sure the other understands what he is saying and why. They don't just scream at each other, but rather they allow each other to explain something and then really try to make sure the other understands him. Also, by staying as calm as he could, Jacob's father was able to articulate why he was upset: because it appeared that Jacob had spent the money without thinking, and because it left him vulnerable in an emergency.

The best scenario is when both the teenager and the parent feel comfortable saying, "No, I really felt this, not what you are saying." That way, both feel free to admit mistakes, clear up misunderstandings, and explain themselves.

Getting a Job

Most parents believe that at some point their teens should have paying jobs. From what we gather, this is not because parents want their teens to "pay their own way," but because they want teens to see for themselves, hands on, that money doesn't grow on trees. Parents want to instill a certain set of values in their kids, and they think getting a job is going to do this.

Well, reality check, it's probably not going to work if we are talking about a job during the school year. While getting a job and learning the value of a dollar sounds great in theory, it's not going to happen just because you decide it's time for that to happen.

We know you were there once, doing the high school thing and whatnot, but there is a big difference between what things were like when you were a teenager and what they're like now. Getting into college now consumes your teenager's life.

On every level, it is harder today to get into a good college than it was when you were a teen. Therefore, it is harder for teens to make time for a job. To teenagers today, it's unreasonable and unfair for parents to ask them to work during the school week and be able to sustain good grades. Whether it truly is unreasonable or unfair, this is how your teen will see it.

Because of the competition to get into college, parents need to decide whether it is more important for their child to learn the value of money or to earn good grades. Yes, it is theoretically possible to do both, but one of those two things needs to be the priority, and the other has to work around it.

Still, many teens do want to work because they feel like having their own money gives them some type of freedom.

The key here is that your teen has to make that decision for himself in order to take away anything valuable from the experience. If your teen feels that his education comes first and you are making him work during the week, the only thing he is going to learn is how to say "I hate my parents" in nine different languages.

You might be thinking to yourself, "Okay, that's during the week, but my teen has plenty of time over the weekend to do his homework and have a job." This might be true, but you really want to stay away from overloading your kid with things to do. It's one thing if your teen overloads his own schedule; it's another if you do it for him. Your teen is going to need some downtime. No, getting a job won't push him over the edge, but a job during junior year, with no free time to just relax, might be too much for your kid to handle. We know that the last thing you want is for your teen to run out of energy right when the end is coming into sight.

Earlier, when your teen is in ninth grade, he might not be so concerned about his academics, which might lead you to think it's the perfect time for him to get a job and learn a lesson or two on money. Wrong. Your teen may not realize that the ninth-grade transcript plays a tremendous part in the college application process, but it does, so you need to help your kid stay focused. As the parent, you need to be the one thinking two steps ahead of the game. You might have to be the one to talk your teenager *out of* getting a job. You certainly have your work cut out for you.

We are not trying to discourage you from helping your teenager get a job. Summer jobs are great; weekend jobs can work well too. We think there is much to be learned from a teen experiencing, instead of hearing, how hard it is to make enough money to buy one meal. We just want parents to be realistic about the time and energy it takes to manage school-work nowadays. If you set the bar too high for your teen, he won't get anything out of the job and his grades will probably suffer because of it. It can get pretty gruesome.

How to Motivate Your Teen to Get a Summer Job

By now you know that teens can be extremely lazy. If you really want your teen to get a summer job, try these steps:

- Make sure he starts looking earlier rather than later . . . jobs can be hard to come by for teenagers.
- Help him decide on the right kind of job for him, something that won't stress him out too much (it's his summer; you don't want him to dread work). Does he want to work with kids? Try getting a job as a camp counselor. Does she like books? Barnes & Noble is the place to be. Are fashion and friends the most important things to her? Sounds like a boutique at the mall is the way to go. Does he talk about going to film school someday? Obviously, the local cineplex is calling his name.
- Try to make this process fun. He will be looking for jobs during the school year. The school year is stressful enough, so help if he's struggling, but make sure you don't end up doing it all for him. He's going to resent and resist the job if he had nothing to do with choosing it.

Teaching Your Teen to Drive

Most of the time, if a teenager gets a job, he's going to need a car. If you're the one who ends up teaching your teen how to drive, it's going to be a stressful experience for both of you, so we've come up with some pointers to make the process as painless as possible.

We know that you are looking out for your teen's safety whenever you scream, *"Oh my God! Stop!"* or *"Watch out!"* from the passenger seat. The problem is that even though screaming is your natural reaction, it can make the situation far worse for your teen.

If you start screaming when nobody is really in danger, your teen is going to get defensive, start screaming back, and lose concentration on the real goal: learning how to drive safely. So bottom line, take a deep breath and relax.

THE PERILS OF PARALLEL PARKING WITH YOUR TEEN

Jed is sixteen and just learning how to drive. His mother, Henrietta, is taking him out to practice on some quiet streets behind their house. They decide to work on parallel parking.

"Okay, Jed, why don't you pull up next to that white car and then park behind it?" Henrietta points to a white van parked on the right. Jed is backing into the space and all of a sudden . . . bump! He hits the curb.

"You're on the curb, Jed!" Henrietta screams.

"Chill out, Mom. I realize that."

"Well, if you hit the curb on your road test you're going to fail."

"As if I don't know this, Mom—"

"So you don't want me to say anything when you mess up? You won't learn anything if I just sit here quietly."

"So be it. You're only in the car because I can't drive without an adult, so please, *stop*."

"Fine, I won't say a word, not a single word. You can't teach yourself, you know. You'll fail if you try to."

When a teen is learning how to drive it can be both really exciting and really stressful. It's your job to keep us confident and safe, but not to criticize when nobody is in danger. For example, it's okay to say, "Don't switch lanes yet. It's not clear," as a helpful hint and a safety precaution, but when you're on an empty street, your teen doesn't need to have you freaking out about every move he makes.

Also, your teen probably knows the facts about getting his license better than you do, so saying things like "If you hit the curb on your road test you're going to fail" is neither an eye-opener for your teen nor is it ultimately helpful. If you say something like this, your teen just becomes frustrated; because he knows this already, he doesn't want to hear it again and again. It will interfere with his ability to concentrate, and he'll probably take out his frustration on you.

We know that it's hard for you to stay relaxed when you see your teen drive, but if you want your teen to be relaxed at the wheel rather than tensed up, try to restrain yourself. Don't yell if you don't have a really good reason to.

A BETTER APPROACH

"Okay, Jed, why don't you pull up next to that white car and then park behind it?" Henrietta points to a white van parked on the right. Jed is backing into the space and all of a sudden . . . bump! He hits the curb.

"You're on the curb, Jed!" Henrietta screams.

"Chill out, Mom. I realize that."

"Okay. Sorry. I know you know that. I just get a little nervous. I can't believe you're driving already, and I worry about your safety, especially when I realize I won't be here in the car with you in case of an emergency."

"Well, get over it. You just make me more nervous when you scream, and I'm worried that you are analyzing every mistake instead of all the good stuff. . . ."

"We all learned to drive at some point, so I know it's hard, and people make mistakes. I'd rather focus on improving your weak spots than concentrate on the things you've already mastered. As you know, all it takes is one mistake and you are in some serious trouble, my friend."

"I get that."

"Right, but it's my job to reiterate it. It's scarier than you can imagine. Now let's try the parking again. This time I'll stay quiet."

It's okay if you freak out at first; it can be hard to hold back, we understand that, but after you get out the initial frustration, you have to pull back and try to breathe, like Henrietta did. Your teen will understand if you freak out, but then they want you to chill out. For example, after Henrietta screams, Jed calms her down ("Chill out, Mom. I realize that") and then Henrietta is able to speak rationally and not make Jed nervous.

The reason Jed doesn't bug her is that he actually feels bad for his mom. He knows that it's probably really hard for her to start to let go, and because she explains this to him he is more willing to move forward instead of making it an enormous and unnecessary issue when she loses it. It was also smart of Henrietta to say, "We all learned to drive at some point, so I know it's hard, and people make mistakes." Often, teens will say, "You literally grew up in a different century, you don't understand," but Henrietta makes it obvious that she learned to drive under the same stress that Jed is experiencing. She even goes a step further and explains why she isn't giving him constant compliments when he's not making mistakes.

A teen always needs to feel secure, and Jed is relying on his mom to make him feel good about his driving. It's smart that Henrietta doesn't constantly throw compliments at him, because when it comes to driving she doesn't want her teen to be overly confident on the road; nothing good can come of that.

Afterword

After reading this book, you are probably thinking you don't stand a chance. Really, we don't think so, either. You don't stand a chance of coming out of your child's teen years the same way you went into them. And you don't stand a chance of making it through with your sanity intact if you don't realize that with all the change going on at your house, you're going to be changing, too.

Like most parents, you probably think that if you just remember what it was like to be a teenager, and apply a firm hand to prevent your teen from making the same mistakes you did, everything will be okay. Well, as usual, you're wrong. Your heart's in the right place, though, and as long as you hold on to that, there is still hope.

As much as teenagers like to give you guys a lot of grief, they still want to come home at the end of the day and hear the words "I love you." Of course, this too takes work, and we're sure to do things that will make "I love you" way down toward the bottom of the list of things you want to say to us when we get home, but if you stay optimistic and make sure your teen does the same, everything will fall into place.

Every parent-teenager relationship hits its fair share of bumps, but the trick is to hold your ground and keep trying. A teen *always* recognizes when a parent is trying to understand him and when a parent doesn't bother to try. This is one of those times when meaning well counts, and if you keep trying, no matter what, you and your teen both have a pretty good chance of coming out the other end in one piece.

Good luck. And remember, it's only seven years of your life.

About the Authors

Photo by Rachel Shapiro

Lara Fox and Hilary Frankel are high school students in New York, New York.